DISMANTLING
SYSTEMIC
RACISM

AND ITS EFFECTS

**INCLUDES TOOLS TO NAVIGATE
WITHIN THE CURRENT SYSTEM**

Dr. Cassundra White-Elliott

DISMANTLING SYSTEMIC RACISM AND ITS EFFECTS

INCLUDES TOOLS TO NAVIGATE WITHIN THE CURRENT SYSTEM

CLF Publishing Collaborative, LLC
Hesperia, CA 92345
Visit us at clfpublishing.org

First Edition: July 2024

Library of Congress Cataloging-in-Publication Data
Names, White-Elliott, Dr. Cassundra, author.
Title: *Dismantling Systemic Racism and Its Effects*
Description: First edition. | Hesperia, California: CLF Publishing Collaborative,
LLC, 2024. | Includes bibliographical references. Audience: Ages 16 and up. |
Summary: *Dismantling Systemic Racism and Its Effects* delivers a powerful
and insightful exploration into the pervasive and enduring impacts of
systemic racism on individuals, communities, and society at large, while
providing readers with a comprehensive understanding of the historical
roots, current manifestations, and far-reaching consequences of systemic
racism. – Provided by publisher.

Identifiers: LCCN 2024910591 |ISBN 9780989235877 (hardcover)
LC record available at https://lccn.loc.gov/2024910591

ISBN 978-0-9892358-7-7 (hardcover)

ACKNOWLEDGEMENTS

To all the authors who are credited in the References section for your contribution to the work in the area of systemic racism and discrimination and in dismantling societal inequities and inequalities.

DEDICATIONS

For everyone who has enough care and
concern to speak out for justice for those
who have been disenfranchised,
marginalized, and discriminated against.

For all students who will peruse the words
upon these pages and whose hearts
will be pricked. Consider yourself
empowered to effectuate change
in your communities.

For everyone in a position of power
who is in the center of the action who
decidedly can and will utilize their
roles to effectuate change in their
communities within education,
government, politics, housing,
healthcare, and the criminal
justice system.

Contents

Introduction
Conceptualizing Systemic Racism

Systemic racism is a pervasive form of racial discrimination and inequality that is deeply ingrained within the structures, policies, and practices of society, perpetuating advantages for some racial groups while disadvantaging others, according to Sandra Smith et al's (2017) research. This form of racism operates at both individual and institutional levels, manifesting in various facets of life, including education, healthcare, employment, criminal justice, housing, and more. Andersen and Collins (2015) surmise that it is not simply a matter of individual prejudice or bias, but rather a broader, interconnected system of oppression that has historical roots and continues to shape the experiences and opportunities of different racial groups today.

At its core, systemic racism stems from historical processes, such as colonialism, slavery, segregation, and discrimination that have marginalized certain racial groups while privileging others postulates Dr. Ibram Kendi (2016). These injustices have left lasting legacies that continue to impact society in profound ways. For example, the legacy of slavery in the United States has led to enduring economic disparities between Black and white Americans, with Black individuals experiencing higher rates of poverty, unemployment, and wealth inequality asserts Jacquelyn Jones (2010).

One key aspect of systemic racism, according to Oakes and Lipton (2003), is its pervasiveness across multiple institutions and sectors of society. In education, for instance, disparities in funding, resources, and disciplinary practices often disadvantage students of color, contributing to achievement gaps and unequal educational outcomes. Similarly, in healthcare, racial biases among healthcare providers, unequal access to quality care, and disparities in health outcomes contribute to poorer health outcomes for many racial minority groups state Williams and Mohammed (2013).

In the realm of employment, systemic racism manifests through hiring discrimination, wage disparities, and limited opportunities for career advancement for people of color according to Pager and Shepherd (2008). Furthermore, studies by Bertrand and Mullainathan (2004) have shown that job applicants with "ethnic-sounding" names are less likely to receive callbacks for interviews compared to those with "white-sounding" names, highlighting the persistence of racial biases in hiring practices.

The criminal justice system is another area where systemic racism is deeply entrenched. Black and brown individuals are disproportionately targeted by law enforcement, subjected to harsher sentencing, and more likely to be incarcerated compared to their white counterparts states Michelle Alexander (2010). Angela Davis (2019) believes this racial bias is evident at every stage of the criminal justice process, from policing and arrests to prosecution and sentencing, leading to mass incarceration and the perpetuation of cycles of poverty and disenfranchisement within communities of color.

Richard Rothstein (2017) asserts systemic racism also plays a significant role in housing and urban development, with practices such as redlining, discriminatory lending practices, and housing segregation contributing to residential segregation and unequal access to housing opportunities for people of color. These practices have profound implications for wealth accumulation, neighborhood quality, and access to resources and opportunities, perpetuating socioeconomic disparities along racial lines.

The media and cultural representations also contribute to systemic racism by perpetuating stereotypes, biases, and narratives that reinforce negative perceptions of people of color while centering whiteness as the norm assert Hall et al. (2013). This can lead to internalized racism and the perpetuation of harmful stereotypes that undermine the dignity and humanity of marginalized communities.

Addressing systemic racism requires a multi-faceted approach that acknowledges its deep-rooted nature and the interconnectedness of its manifestations across various institutions and systems. Eduardo Bonilla-Silva (2017) suggests this involves not only dismantling discriminatory policies and practices but also addressing the underlying structural inequalities and power dynamics that perpetuate racial disparities. This includes investing in equitable education, healthcare, employment, and housing opportunities, as well as implementing policies that promote racial justice, diversity, and inclusion.

Moreover, Robin DiAngelo (2018) posits combating systemic racism requires confronting implicit biases and challenging the narratives and representations that reinforce racial stereotypes and inequalities. This involves fostering dialogue and understanding across racial lines, as well as amplifying the voices and experiences of marginalized communities.

Ultimately, achieving racial equity and justice requires a commitment to dismantling systemic racism at its roots and building a more inclusive and equitable society where all individuals have the opportunity to thrive regardless of their race or ethnicity. This necessitates sustained effort, advocacy, and collective action to address the systemic injustices that continue to shape our world today.

1
Critical Race
Theory

1
Unveiling the Dynamics of Critical Race Theory: A Comprehensive Overview

This chapter investigates the intricacies of Critical Race Theory (CRT), a framework developed within legal studies that analyzes how race intersects with societal structures to perpetuate systemic inequality. The research will elucidate CRT's origin, foundational principles, key concepts, central tenets, applications, and critiques. The purpose of examining CRT's implications across various disciplines is to provide a comprehensive understanding of its significance in contemporary discourse.

Origins and Development of Critical Race Theory
CRT emerged in the late 20th century as a response to the limitations of traditional civil rights approaches that failed to address the persistence of racial inequality in society. Rooted in legal scholarship, CRT offers a multidisciplinary lens through which to analyze the intricate interplay between race, power, and law in society and to influence increased discourse in various academic disciplines and social movements.

Delgado and Stefancic's (2017) research asserts, CRT emerged in the 1970s and 1980s, building upon the insights of earlier civil rights movements and legal scholarship, tracing its roots to the pioneering works of legal scholars, including Derrick Bell, Kimberlé Crenshaw, and Richard Delgado, along with educational theorist Gloria Ladson-Billings, who all sought to challenge the prevailing narrative of colorblindness and advocate for a more complete understanding of racism and its effects. Drawing inspiration from Critical Legal Studies, which critiqued the neutrality of law; the Black Power movement, which emphasized the need for structural change to address racial injustice; feminist theory; and postcolonial studies, CRT evolved into a distinct theoretical framework that interrogates the role of race in shaping social structures and institutions.

Key Concepts of Critical Race Theory
1. Intersectionality: CRT emphasizes the inter-sectional nature of oppression, highlighting how race intersects with other forms of identity such as gender, class, and sexuality according to Crenshaw's (1989) research. This inter-sectional approach acknowledges the unique experiences of individuals who navigate mul-tiple marginalized identities and underscores the importance of addressing intersecting forms of discrimination.
2. Permanence of Racism: According to Delgado and Stefancic's research from 2017, contrary to notions of post-racialism (the belief that racial prejudices and discrimination no longer exist), CRT posits that racism is not a tem-porary aberration but is deeply embedded in the fabric of society and persists despite legal and social advances. By recognizing the enduring nature of racism, CRT challenges complacency and calls for sustained efforts to dismantle systemic inequalities.
3. Social Construction of Race: According to Delgado and Stefancic (2017), CRT rejects biological determinism and contends that race is a socially constructed concept with real-world implications. By deconstructing essen-tialist notions of race, CRT unveils the historical and political processes that shape racial identities and hierarchies.
4. Interest Convergence: Bell's 1980 study demonstrates CRT suggests that racial pro-gress often occurs when it aligns with the

interests of dominant groups. This theory high-lights the instrumental nature of racial reforms and underscores the importance of coalition-building and strategic alliances in advancing social justice agendas.

5. Critical Pedagogy: Ladson-Billings' 1998 study reveals CRT extends beyond legal scholarship with the purpose of informing critical peda-gogical practices aimed at challenging domi-nant narratives and empowering marginalized communities. By centering the voices and experiences of people of color in educational settings, CRT seeks to foster critical con-sciousness and promote social transformation while challenging dominant narratives of race and racism.

Central Tenets of Critical Race Theory

1. Race as a Social Construct: Delgado and Stefancic postulate CRT rejects essentialist views of race and instead emphasizes its fluid and contingent nature. Race is understood as a product of social interactions, historical con-text, and power dynamics rather than inherent biological traits. By interrogating the social, political, and historical dimensions of race, CRT unveils the arbitrary nature of racial cate-gories and exposes the mechanisms of raciali-zation.

2. Intersectional Analysis: CRT advocates for an intersectional analysis that recognizes the interconnectedness of race, gender, class, and other forms of identity, according to Crenshaw. By examining how multiple forms of oppression intersect, CRT provides a more comprehensive understanding of systemic inequalities and informs strategies for social change.

3. Critique of Liberal Legalism: CRT critiques liberal legal frameworks for their failure to address the root causes of racial inequality postulate Delgado and Stefancic. CRT critiques mainstream legal approaches for their failure to address systemic racism.
    It challenges the neutrality of law and argues that legal institutions often perpetuate racial inequality through their structure and application.
4. Narrative of Colorblindness (Counter storytelling): Delgado and Stefancic's research suggests CRT rejects colorblind approaches to race that ignore the continued significance of race in shaping societal outcomes.
    It argues that colorblindness perpetuates racial inequality by masking systemic discrimination and hindering efforts to address it. CRT promotes the use of counter storytelling as a method of resistance and empowerment. By elevating the voices and narratives of marginalized communities, CRT challenges dominant narratives of race and racism and disrupts hegemonic power structures.

Criticisms of Critical Race Theory

Despite its contributions to scholarship and activism, CRT has faced criticism from various factions.

1. Essentialism: Critics argue that CRT's emphasis on race, as a central organizing principle, risks essentializing racial identity and overlooking other forms of social identity and oppression.
2. Determinism: Some critics contend that CRT's focus on the permanence of racism and the role of structures and institutions in perpetuating inequality can lead to determinism and

a sense of hopelessness about the possibility of social change.
3. Political Controversy: CRT has become a subject of political controversy, with critics accusing it of promoting divisive ideologies and undermining traditional liberal values, such as equality and individualism.

Applications of Critical Race Theory
1. Legal Scholarship: CRT has had a profound impact on legal scholarship, particularly in areas such as constitutional law, criminal justice, and employment discrimination suggests Delgado and Stefancic. By exposing the racial biases inherent in legal doctrines and institutions, CRT has influenced legal arguments and advocacy strategies aimed at addressing systemic racism within the legal system in the pursuit of racial justice.
2. Education: Ladson-Billings' research suggests CRT has been applied to the field of education to address racial disparities in academic achievement, discipline practices, curriculum development, access to educational opportunities. By integrating CRT principles into educational pedagogy, practitioners seek to create inclusive learning environments that empower students from diverse racial and cultural backgrounds.
3. Social Justice Activism: CRT has informed social justice activism aimed at dismantling systemic racism and advancing racial equity, by addressing systemic racism in various domains, including housing, healthcare, and environmental justice stipulates Delgado and Stefancic. By mobilizing grassroots movements and advocating for policy reforms, activists draw upon CRT principles to

challenge institutionalized forms of discrimination and promote transformative change.

Critical Race Theory offers a powerful framework for understanding the complex ways in which race intersects with systems of power and privilege in society. By centering the experiences of marginalized communities and challenging dominant narratives of race and racism, CRT provides valuable insights for addressing systemic inequality and advancing social justice by shedding light on the enduring legacies of racial injustice and informing efforts to create a more just and equitable world.

2

Policies of Yesteryear

.

2
Policies of Yesteryear
(Attempts to Dismantle Systemic Racism)

Though systemic racism has deep historical roots in the United States (existing well before the establishment of the thirteen colonies), persisting across centuries and permeating societal structures, concerted efforts have been made through policies, programs, and laws to combat its pervasive influence. These initiatives span across multiple sectors, addressing disparities in education, employment, housing, criminal justice, health, and economic empowerment. While this list is not exhaustive, it highlights key examples of interventions aimed at dismantling systemic racism and advancing equity.

Equal Protection Clause of the 14th Amendment

The Equal Protection Clause, found in the 14th Amendment to the United States Constitution, is a fundamental principle of American law that prohibits states from denying any person within their jurisdiction the equal protection of the laws. The clause states: "No State shall... deny to any person within its jurisdiction the equal protection of the laws." The clause was ratified in 1868 as part of the Reconstruction Amendments following the Civil War. The 14th Amendment was intended to ensure civil rights and equal protection under the law for all citizens, particularly formerly enslaved individuals and other marginalized groups. The Equal Protection Clause applies to all levels of government, including state and local governments, and prohibits discrimination on the basis of race, ethnicity, gender, religion, and other protected characteristics. The Equal Protection Clause has been central to many landmark Supreme Court decisions, including Brown v. Board of Education (1954), which declared state laws establishing separate public schools for black and white students unconstitutional. Over time, the Equal Protection Clause has been interpreted to protect a wide range of rights, including the right to marry, access to education, voting rights, and reproductive rights. Despite legal protections, challenges to equal protection persist, including issues of racial profiling, unequal treatment in the criminal justice system, disparities in educational opportunities, and barriers to voting rights. The Equal Protection Clause of the 14th Amendment is a cornerstone of American civil rights law, prohibiting discrimination and ensuring equal treatment under the law for all individuals.

Civil Rights Act of 1964
The Civil Rights Act of 1964 was a landmark piece of legislation that marked a significant step forward in the struggle for civil rights and equality in the United States. It helped dismantle the legal framework of segregation and discrimination, paved the way for greater equality and opportunity, and served as a model for subsequent civil rights legislation. The Act remains one of the most important and enduring achievements of the Civil Rights Movement.

Here is a summary of its key provisions and significance:

- Title I: Desegregation of Public Facilities: Title I of the Civil Rights Act prohibited discrimination in public accommodations, such as hotels, restaurants, theaters, and other establishments engaged in interstate commerce. It ended segregation in these places and ensured equal access for all individuals, regardless of race or ethnicity.
- Title II: Equal Employment Opportunity: Title II of the Civil Rights Act prohibited employment discrimination based on race, color, religion, sex, or national origin. It established the Equal Employment Opportunity Commission (EEOC)

to enforce these provisions and investigate claims of discrimination in the workplace.

- Title III: Desegregation of Public Education: Title III of the Civil Rights Act authorized the federal government to withhold funds from public schools that continued to practice segregation. It paved the way for the desegregation of schools and the integration of students of different races.

- Title IV: Desegregation of Public Facilities Receiving Federal Funding: Title IV of the Civil Rights Act prohibited discrimination in federally funded programs and activities, including schools, hospitals, and public housing. It ensured that institutions receiving federal funds could not discriminate based on race, color, religion, sex, or national origin.

- Title V: Commission on Civil Rights: Title V of the Civil Rights Act established the United States Commission on Civil Rights to investigate complaints of discrimination and recommend policies to address civil rights issues.

- Title VI: Non-Discrimination in Federally Assisted Programs: Title VI of the Civil Rights Act prohibited discrimination based on race, color, or national origin in programs and activities receiving federal financial assistance. It ensured that recipients of federal funds did not engage in discriminatory practices.

- Title VII: Equal Employment Opportunity Commission (EEOC): Title VII of the Civil Rights Act, under the jurisdiction of the EEOC, prohibits discrimination in employment on the basis of race, color, religion, sex, or national origin. It prohibits practices such as hiring, firing, promotion, and compensation discrimination.

Education

Brown v. Board of Education (1954)

Prior to Brown v. Board of Education, racial segregation in public schools was common, upheld by the 1896 Supreme Court decision in Plessy v. Ferguson, which established the "separate but equal" doctrine. This doctrine allowed for segregation as long as the facilities for black and white students were purportedly equal. Brown v. Board of Education origi-nated in Topeka, Kansas, where Linda Brown, a black third-grader, had to travel a significant distance to attend a segregated black school despite a white school being much closer to her home. Her father, Oliver Brown, was one of several plaintiffs in a class-action suit filed by the NAACP against the Board of Education of Topeka, challenging the constitutionality of racial segregation in public schools.

The case was initially heard in the U.S. District Court for the District of Kansas, which upheld the segregation, citing the Plessy precedent. The case was then appealed to the Supreme Court, where it was combined with other similar cases from South Carolina, Virginia, Delaware, and Washington, D.C. The plaintiffs, represented by NAACP lawyers including Thurgood Marshall, argued that segregated schools were inherently unequal and violated the Equal Protec-tion Clause of the 14th Amendment. The defense argued that segregation was a long-standing practice and that states should have the authority to regulate their own education systems.

On May 17, 1954, the Supreme Court, led by Chief Justice Earl Warren, delivered a unanimous 9-0 decision in favor of the plaintiffs. The Court held that "separate educational facilities are inherently unequal," overturning Plessy v. Ferguson in the context of public education. The Court found segregation in public schools instilled a sense of inferiority among black children that undermined their educational opportunities and personal growth. The decision was a landmark victory for the Civil Rights Movement, setting a legal precedent for challenging segregation and discrimination. It paved the way for further civil rights advancements, including the Civil Rights Act of 1964 and the Voting Rights Act of 1965. Despite the ruling, many schools and communities resisted desegregation, leading to a series of legal battles and federal interventions throughout the 1960s and beyond.

Over time, however, Brown v. Board of Education significantly contributed to the dismantling of institutionalized racial segregation in the United States. Brown v. Board of Education remains one of the most pivotal Supreme Court cases in American history, symbolizing the judiciary's role in advancing civil rights and equality. Brown v. Board of Education (1954) was a transformative Supreme Court decision that declared state laws establishing separate public schools for black and white students to be unconstitutional, marking a significant victory in the fight against systemic racism and setting the stage for further civil rights advancements. It underscored the importance of the Equal Protection Clause and set a precedent for future rulings against discriminatory practices.

While Brown v. Board of Education was a major step forward, achieving true educational equity remains an ongoing challenge. Issues such as de facto segregation, disparities in school funding, and unequal access to resources continue to affect minority students.

Elementary and Secondary Education Act (ESEA) of 1965

The Elementary and Secondary Education Act (ESEA) of 1965 was a landmark legislation aimed at reducing educational disparities by providing federal funding to support schools serving low-income students. It established a framework for federal involvement in education, promoting equity and setting the stage for future educational reforms and policies. Prior to the ESEA, educational funding in the United States was largely decentralized, with significant disparities in resources between affluent and impoverished areas. This often resulted in inequitable educational opportunities, particularly for students in low-income and minority communities. President Lyndon B. Johnson, as part of his "War on Poverty" and broader Great Society initiatives, aimed to address these disparities by providing federal support to improve education for disadvantaged students.

The most significant and well-known component of the ESEA, Title I provides financial assistance to local educational agencies (LEAs) and schools with high numbers or high percentages of children from low-income families. The goal is to ensure that all children meet challenging state academic standards. ESEA significantly increased federal funding for education, with funds distributed based on formulas that considered the number of low-income students in each district. By providing additional resources to schools serving disadvantaged students, the act sought to close achievement gaps and promote educational equity.

As a major reauthorization of ESEA, No Child Left Behind (NCLB) Act of 2001 emphasized standardized testing, accountability, and closing achievement gaps. It mandated annual testing, academic progress tracking, and consequences for schools failing to make adequate yearly progress. Replacing NCLB, Every Student Succeeds Act (ESSA) of 2015 returned more control to states while maintaining a focus on accountability and equity. It provided states with greater flexibility in designing accountability systems and interventions for underperforming schools. ESEA laid the groundwork for federal involvement in ensuring educational equity, particularly for low-income and minority students.

While ESEA has provided critical funding, disparities in educational resources persist, often influenced by local and state funding variations. The act's successive reauthorizations reflect ongoing efforts to address educational challenges, adapt to new priorities, and improve educational outcomes for all students.

Extended Opportunity Programs & Services (EOPS)

Extended Opportunity Programs and Services (EOPS) aims to support low-income and educationally disadvantaged students in achieving their educational goals, such as obtaining an associate degree, vocational certificate, or transferring to a four-year university. The program specifically targets students who face economic and educational barriers to higher education. EOPS provides personalized academic, career, and personal counseling to help students develop and follow an educational plan and offers tutoring services in various subjects to help students improve their academic performance. EOPS provides financial assistance in the form of grants and book vouchers to help cover the costs of tuition, textbooks, and other educational expenses.

Students in EOPS receive priority registration, allowing them to enroll in classes before general registration begins. This helps ensure they get the courses they need to stay on track with their educational plans. EOPS offers workshops on study skills, time management, financial literacy, and other topics to help students succeed academically and personally; provides resources and guidance for students planning to transfer to four-year institutions, including transfer fairs and application assistance; creates a supportive community through mentoring programs and peer support networks, fostering a sense of belonging and motivation among students.

The program's comprehensive approach addresses both academic and personal challenges, helping students navigate and succeed in higher education. EOPS promotes educational equity by providing targeted support to students who might otherwise be unable to pursue or complete their higher education goals. EOPS is available in community colleges across California, consistently evolving to meet the changing needs of students. The program is widely recognized for its effectiveness in supporting disadvantaged students and has served as a model for similar programs in other states.

Employment

Equal Employment Opportunity Commission (EEOC)

The Equal Employment Opportunity Commission (EEOC) was established by the Civil Rights Act of 1964. The EEOC is responsible for enforcing federal laws that prohibit employment discrimination based on race, color, religion, sex (including pregnancy, gender identity, and sexual orientation), national origin, age (40 or older), disability, and genetic information. The EEOC plays a critical role in promoting fairness and equality in the workplace by addressing and mitigating discriminatory practices. The EEOC investigates discrimination complaints filed by employees or job applicants. It assesses whether there is reasonable cause to believe that discrimination has occurred. The EEOC offers mediation as a voluntary process for resolving disputes before a formal investigation. If discrimination is found, the EEOC attempts to settle the charge through conciliation. If conciliation efforts fail, the EEOC may file a lawsuit against employers to enforce anti-discrimination laws. It can also intervene in private lawsuits.

Through its litigation efforts, the EEOC has helped establish important legal precedents that shape anti-discrimination law and policy. The EEOC provides a vital resource for workers facing discrimination, offering avenues for redress, and promoting a more inclusive work environment. The EEOC provides guidance on anti-discrimination laws and conducts outreach and education programs to help employers and employees understand their rights and responsibilities. The EEOC develops regulations and policies to interpret and enforce anti-discrimination laws effectively. Major laws enforced by the EEOC include Title VII of the Civil Rights Act of 1964; Age Discrimination in Employment Act (ADEA) of 1967; Americans with Disabilities Act (ADA) of 1990; and Genetic Information Nondiscrimination Act (GINA) of 2008.

Affirmative Action Programs

Affirmative action programs aim to address historical and systemic discrimination by promoting diversity and equality in education, employment, and contracting. The primary goals are to increase opportunities for underrepresented minorities, women, and other disadvantaged groups, ensuring fair treatment and equal access to opportunities. Affirmative action has increased diversity in schools, workplaces, and government contracting. It has helped create opportunities for individuals from historically marginalized groups, contributing to social and economic mobility. Affirmative action policies in higher education seek to diversify student bodies by considering race, ethnicity, and other factors as part of a holistic admissions process. Some programs offer financial assistance specifically for minority students to enhance their access to higher education.

Employers implement affirmative action plans to ensure diverse applicant pools and fair hiring practices. This may include targeted outreach and recruitment efforts to attract candidates from underrepresented groups. Affirmative action in employment also involves creating opportunities for advancement and professional development for minorities and women.

Critics argue that affirmative action can lead to reverse discrimination, unfairly disadvantaging majority groups. Legal challenges have led to limitations and bans on affirmative action in some states through voter referenda and court rulings. The debate over affirmative action continues, with discussions focusing on the balance between achieving diversity and ensuring fairness for all individuals. The use of affirmative action in college admissions is frequently reviewed and litigated. Some states have banned race-based affirmative action through voter initiatives. Affirmative action remains a requirement for federal contractors, with ongoing efforts to promote workplace diversity.

Housing

Fair Housing Act of 1968
The Fair Housing Act was enacted in the aftermath of the Civil Rights Movement to address widespread housing discrimination and segregation. The primary goal is to eliminate discrimination in housing based on race, color, religion, sex, national origin, familial status, or disability, ensuring equal housing opportunities for all. It is illegal to refuse to sell or rent a dwelling to any person because of race, color, religion, sex, national origin, familial status, or disability. The FHA prohibits making, printing, or publishing any notice, statement, or advertisement that indicates any preference, limitation, or discrimination based on these protected

characteristics. FHA outlaws discrimination in mortgage lending and other financial services related to housing. FHA bans discrimination by real estate agents and brokers in providing services related to buying, selling, or renting homes.

Individuals who believe they have been discriminated against can file a complaint with the Department of Housing and Urban Development (HUD), which investigates complaints and, if necessary, refers cases to the Department of Justice (DOJ) for further action. The Act has played a crucial role in promoting residential integration and combating segregation. Numerous court cases have interpreted and enforced the Act, helping to clarify its provisions and strengthen protections. Despite the Act's provisions, enforcement has been inconsistent, and discrimination persists in some areas. Structural barriers, such as zoning laws and economic disparities, continue to contribute to segregated housing patterns.

The Fair Housing Act is a landmark piece of civil rights legislation that has significantly advanced the cause of equal housing opportunity. The Act remains a critical tool in addressing housing discrimination and promoting fair housing practices in the United States.

Criminal Justice

Voting Rights Act of 1965

The Voting Rights Act (VRA) of 1965 was enacted during the Civil Rights Movement to address discriminatory voting practices that disenfranchised African Americans and other minority groups. The primary goal of the VRA was to eliminate barriers to voting and ensure that all citizens, regardless of race or ethnicity, had equal access to the ballot box.

Section 2 prohibits any voting practice or procedure that discriminates on the basis of race, color, or language minority status. Section 4 established a formula to identify jurisdictions with a history of discriminatory voting practices, subjecting them to federal oversight. Section 5 defines the "preclearance" requirement mandated that jurisdictions with a history of discrimination obtain federal approval before making any changes to their voting laws or procedures.

The VRA led to a significant increase in voter registration and turnout among African Americans and other minority groups, particularly in Southern states where discriminatory practices were prevalent. By eliminating barriers to voting, the VRA facilitated the election of minority candidates to public office at all levels of government. The VRA set a powerful legal precedent for combating voting discrimination and protecting voting rights as fundamental to American democracy. In this landmark Supreme Court case, the Court struck down the coverage formula in Section 4(b) of the VRA, effectively invalidating the preclearance requirement. This decision led to concerns about the resurgence of voting discrimination in previously covered jurisdictions.

Despite setbacks, efforts to strengthen voting rights and restore key provisions of the VRA, such as preclearance, continue through legislative proposals and legal advocacy. The Voting Rights Act of 1965 is widely regarded as one of the most significant achievements of the Civil Rights Movement, marking a transformative moment in American history. While significant progress has been made, ongoing challenges, such as voter suppression efforts and gerrymandering, highlight the continued need to protect and expand voting rights for all Americans.

Fair Sentencing Act of 2010

The Fair Sentencing Act of 2010 was enacted to reduce the significant disparities between sentences for crack and powder cocaine offenses, which disproportionately affected African American communities. Prior to the Act, the sentencing disparity was 100:1, meaning possession of just 5 grams of crack cocaine triggered the same mandatory minimum sentence as 500 grams of powder cocaine. The Act reduced this disparity to 18:1 by increasing the amount of crack cocaine necessary to trigger mandatory minimum sentences. Specifically, it raised the threshold for a five-year minimum sentence from 5 grams to 28 grams and for a ten-year minimum sentence from 50 grams to 280 grams. Additionally, the Act eliminated the mandatory minimum sentence for simple possession of crack cocaine. These changes aimed to create a fairer and more equitable criminal justice system by addressing racial inequalities and promoting more proportionate sentencing practices.

Health

Affordable Care Act (ACA) of 2010

The Affordable Care Act (ACA), signed into law in 2010 under the Obama administration, represents a comprehensive overhaul of the American healthcare system aimed at expanding access to healthcare, controlling healthcare costs, and improving the quality of care. The ACA required most Americans to obtain health insurance coverage or pay a penalty, aiming to increase the number of insured individuals and spread the risk pool among health insurers, ensuring not one group received all the healthy individuals. The law established state-based and federally facilitated health insurance exchanges, where individuals and small businesses could shop for and compare private health insurance plans, often with subsidies to make coverage more affordable. The ACA expanded Medicaid eligibility to cover more low-income adults, providing federal funding to states to extend coverage to individuals earning up to 138% of the federal poverty level. The law prohibited insurance companies from denying coverage or charging higher premiums based on pre-existing conditions, ensuring that individuals with pre-existing health conditions could not be denied coverage or charged exorbitant rates. The ACA mandated that all health insurance plans cover essential health benefits, including preventive care, maternity care, mental health services, and prescription drugs, to ensure comprehensive coverage for consumers. The law allowed young adults to stay on their parents' health insurance plans until age 26, providing a safety net for young adults transitioning into the workforce or pursuing higher education.

Economic Empowerment

Minority Business Development Agency (MBDA)
The Minority Business Development Agency (MBDA) is a federal agency dedicated to promoting the growth and competitiveness of minority-owned businesses in the United States. The MBDA's mission is to foster the growth and global competitiveness of minority-owned businesses by providing access to capital, contracts, and markets. It aims to strengthen minority-owned businesses and create jobs in minority communities. The MBDA offers a range of programs and services to assist minority-owned businesses in various stages of development. The MBDA operates a network of Minority Business Development Centers (MBDCs) across the country, as well as Native American Business Enterprise Centers (NABECs) and Business Enterprise Centers (BECs), which provide specialized assistance to minority-owned businesses in specific industries or regions.

The MBDA conducts outreach and advocacy efforts to raise awareness of the contributions of minority-owned businesses to the economy and to advocate for policies and programs that support their growth and success. It also works to promote supplier diversity and inclusion in corporate procurement practices. The MBDA collaborates with federal, state, and local government agencies, as well as private sector organizations, educational institutions, and community-based organizations, leveraging resources and support the development of minority-owned businesses. The MBDA has a track record of success in helping minority-owned businesses grow and thrive. Its programs and services have helped create jobs, generate economic growth, and promote wealth creation in minority communities across the United States.

Small Business Administration (SBA) 8(a) Business Development Program

The Small Business Administration (SBA) 8(a) Business Development Program is a federal initiative designed to assist small, disadvantaged businesses in gaining access to government contracting oppor-tunities. The primary goal of the 8(a) Program is to promote the growth and development of small businesses owned and operated by individuals who are socially and economically disadvantaged. This includes individuals who are members of minority groups, women, veterans, and individuals from economically disadvantaged communities.

Participation in the 8(a) Program is limited to a maximum of nine years, with a four-year develop-mental stage followed by a five-year transitional stage. The 8(a) Program has been instrumental in helping many small, disadvantaged businesses grow and succeed in the federal marketplace, leading to job creation, economic growth, and increased opportu-nities for socially and economically disadvantaged individuals.

3
Systemic Racism
in Education

3
The Impacts of Systemic Racism on Education

Education is widely regarded as the cornerstone of societal progress and individual opportunity. However, despite significant strides in educational attainment and access, persistent disparities continue to plague the education system, disproportionately affecting marginalized communities, particularly those consisting of Black, Indigenous, and people of color (BIPOC) individuals. Anderson (2015) posits systemic racism in education refers to the ways in which racial discrimination and inequality are embedded within the structures, policies, and practices of educational institutions, perpetuating advantages for some racial groups while disadvantaging others. Howard (2010) suggests this form of racism operates at both individual and institutional levels, manifesting in various aspects of education, including funding, curriculum, discipline, and access to resources and opportunities. The impacts of systemic racism in education are ubiquitous and multifaceted, affecting students, educators, families, and communities, perpetuating racial disparities in academic achievement, social mobility, and life outcomes indicates Ladson-Billings (2006).

This chapter provides a comprehensive analysis of the impacts of systemic racism on education. It examines the various mechanisms through which systemic racism operates in educational institutions, policies, and practices, and explores its implications for BIPOC students. Moreover, it discusses the long-term consequences of these disparities for academic achievement, graduation rates, access to higher education, and socioeconomic mobility. Finally, this chapter discusses strategies and interventions aimed at addressing systemic racism in education and promoting racial equity and social justice.

Disparities in Funding and Resources

Disparities in funding and resources within the education system represent one of the most glaring manifestations of systemic racism. From unequal distribution of financial resources to disparities in school facilities, these inequities have profound implications for academic achievement and long-term socioeconomic outcomes. Downey and Pribesh's (2004) research shows schools with higher proportions of BIPOC students tend to receive fewer resources, including lower per-pupil funding, less experienced teachers, outdated facilities, and limited access to advanced coursework and extracurricular activities. These disparities contribute to unequal educational opportunities and hinder the academic success and social mobility of minority students according to Ferguson's (2001) research.

To understand the contemporary landscape of educational disparities, it is imperative to contextualize them within a historical framework marked by systemic racism. Throughout American history, policies and practices (such as segregation, redlining, and discriminatory funding mechanisms) have systematically marginalized BIPOC communities, perpetuating intergenerational cycles of poverty and inequality according to Orfield and Lee (2005).

For example, the landmark Supreme Court decision in Brown v. Board of Education (1954) ostensibly ended legal segregation in schools. However, the subsequent phenomenon of "white flight" and the proliferation of de facto segregation (non-legislative segregation) through zoning and districting policies undermined the intent of desegregation efforts, perpetuating disparities in resources and opportunities state Orfield and Eaton (1996).

Moreover, the legacy of redlining, which systematically denied mortgage loans and investment to Black communities, resulted in stark disparities in property tax revenue -the primary source of funding for public schools- further exacerbating funding inequities found Rothstein (2017). These historical injustices continue to reverberate throughout the education system, shaping patterns of resource allocation and perpetuating disparities along racial lines.

Despite legal strides towards desegregation and equity in education, disparities in funding and resources persist, reflecting deeply entrenched systemic inequalities. According to a report by the U.S. Government Accountability Office (2018), high-poverty schools serving predominantly Black and Latinx students receive significantly less funding than schools serving predominantly white students, exacerbating resource disparities and limiting opportunities for academic success.

The underfunding of schools in marginalized communities is further compounded by disparities in teacher quality and school infrastructure. Ladson-Billings' (2006) research has consistently shown that schools in low-income neighborhoods are more likely to employ inexperienced teachers and lack access to essential resources such as advanced coursework, extracurricular activities, and modern facilities.

Moreover, the overreliance on property taxes as a primary funding source for public education perpetuates inequalities, as communities with lower property values -often BIPOC communities- struggle to generate adequate revenue for their schools according to Baker and Welner (2011). This creates a vicious cycle of underinvestment, wherein schools in marginalized communities are deprived of the resources necessary to provide a quality education, further perpetuating socioeconomic disparities.

The consequences of disparities in funding and resources within the education system are far-reaching and profound, perpetuating cycles of poverty and marginalization. Academic achievement gaps persist along racial lines, with BIPOC students consistently lagging behind their white counterparts in standardized test scores, graduation rates, and college readiness asserts Reardon (2011).

Moreover, the disparities in educational opportunities perpetuate broader socioeconomic inequalities, limiting the upward mobility and economic prospects of marginalized communities. Bartik and Lachowska's (2012) research indicates that students who attend underfunded schools are less likely to enroll in college, secure stable employment, and achieve financial security, perpetuating intergenerational cycles of poverty and marginalization.

Furthermore, Bonilla-Silva (2017) posits the lack of access to quality education contributes to the perpetuation of systemic racism, as it reinforces stereotypes and structural barriers that impede the social and economic advancement of BIPOC communities. By perpetuating disparities in educational outcomes, systemic racism undermines the principles of equality and opportunity enshrined in the American ethos, perpetuating social stratification and injustice.

One example of the disparity in funding and resources in education is the case of the Detroit Public Schools (DPS) in Michigan. The DPS has long struggled with inadequate funding, crumbling infrastructure, and resource shortages, particularly in comparison to neighboring suburban school districts.

Research conducted by the American Civil Liberties Union (ACLU) of Michigan found significant disparities in the quality of education and resources between DPS and wealthier suburban districts according to American Civil Liberties Union of Michigan (2018).

For example, DPS schools often lack basic amenities, such as functioning heating and cooling systems, updated textbooks, and adequate classroom supplies. Many school buildings are in a state of disrepair, with issues such as leaking roofs, mold infestations, and deteriorating facilities compromising the learning environment for students American Civil Liberties Union of Michigan (2018).

In contrast, neighboring suburban districts benefit from higher property tax revenues, which translate into better-funded schools with modern facilities, well-equipped classrooms, and a wider range of educational opportunities for students. These districts are able to attract and retain highly qualified teachers, offer advanced coursework and extracurricular activities, and provide comprehensive support services to meet the diverse needs of students American Civil Liberties Union of Michigan (2018).

Students attending underfunded schools like those in the DPS are denied access to the resources and opportunities necessary for academic success and personal growth. The case of the Detroit Public Schools exemplifies the lived experience of disparity in funding and resources in education. Addressing these disparities requires systemic reforms to ensure equitable funding distribution, resource allocation, and support for all students, regardless of their socioeconomic background or zip code.

Addressing disparities in funding and resources within the education system requires a multi-faceted approach that addresses both the systemic root causes and immediate consequences of inequality. Policymakers, educators, and community stake-holders must collaborate to implement targeted interventions aimed at promoting equity and inclusivity in education.

One key intervention is the reform of school funding mechanisms to reduce reliance on property taxes and ensure equitable distribution of resources.

Implementing weighted funding formulas that allocate additional resources to high-needs schools and districts can help mitigate disparities and provide all students with access to quality education assert Baker and Corcoran (2012).

Additionally, recruiting and retaining diverse and high-quality teachers is essential for promoting equitable educational outcomes. Investing in teacher training programs, providing competitive salaries, and creating supportive work environments can help attract and retain talented educators in high-needs schools, thereby improving academic outcomes for marginalized students suggest Ingersoll and May (2011).

Furthermore, Noguera (2008) asserts community engagement and empowerment are critical for addressing disparities in education. Building partnerships between schools, families, and community organizations can facilitate holistic support systems that address the social, emotional, and academic needs of students in marginalized communities.

Disparities in funding and resources within the education system represent a pervasive and entrenched manifestation of systemic racism, perpetuating cycles of inequality and marginalization. Historical injustices, discriminatory policies, and socioeconomic factors have contributed to the perpetuation of these disparities, limiting opportunities for academic achievement and socioeconomic mobility among BIPOC communities.

Racial Bias in Discipline

Racial bias within educational institutions manifests through disparities in disciplinary practices and the perpetuation of stereotypes that marginalize minority students. According to Skiba et al. (2002), studies have shown that students of color are more likely to be suspended, expelled, or referred to law enforcement for disciplinary infractions compared to their white counterparts, even for similar behaviors. This punitive approach to discipline contributes to the school-to-prison pipeline and undermines the educational experiences of BIPOC students but also perpetuates cycles of incarceration and marginalization within communities, while perpetuating racial inequalities in academic achievement and life outcomes state Morris and Perry (2016).

The roots of systemic racism in education can be traced back to the historical legacy of slavery, segregation, and discriminatory policies that have systematically marginalized communities of color. Throughout American history, racial segregation in schools, such as the "separate but equal" doctrine upheld by the Supreme Court in Plessy v. Ferguson (1896), perpetuated disparities in educational opportunities along racial lines found Orfield and Eaton (1996).

Moreover, according to Howard (2010), the perpetuation of stereotypes and implicit biases within educational settings contributes to the marginalization of BIPOC students, impacting their self-esteem, academic aspirations, and sense of belonging. Stereotypes regarding intellectual ability, behavior, and cultural competence can influence teacher expectations, classroom dynamics, and academic tracking practices, further exacerbating disparities in educational outcomes.

Furthermore, the psychological toll of racial bias and discrimination within educational settings can have profound implications for the well-being and academic success of BIPOC students. Experiences of stereotypes, racial microaggressions, and institutional racism contribute to feelings of alienation, stress, and disengagement, hindering academic performance and educational attainment purport Sue et al. (2007).

One example of racial bias in school discipline is the case of Kiera Wilmot, a Black teenage girl who faced severe disciplinary action for a science experiment gone wrong. In 2013, Kiera, a 16-year-old student at Bartow High School in Florida, conducted a science experiment in which she mixed household chemicals in a plastic bottle, causing a small explosion. The experiment was conducted outside of school hours, on school grounds, and without any intent to cause harm or disruption.

However, instead of being recognized for her curiosity and initiative in conducting a scientific experiment, Kiera was arrested, charged with felonies, and expelled from school. The incident received widespread media attention, sparking outrage and criticism of the school's disproportionate response to Kiera's actions.

Kiera's case highlights the racial bias and systemic inequities present in school discipline practices. Black students like Kiera are disproportionately subjected to harsh disciplinary measures, such as suspensions, expulsions, and involvement with law enforcement, compared to their white counterparts states Losen and Martinez (2013). These disparities persist even when controlling for factors such as socioeconomic status and school characteristics, indicating the presence of implicit bias and discriminatory practices within the education system.

Furthermore, the consequences of harsh disciplinary actions extend beyond the immediate impact on individual students. Excessive punishment can disrupt students' academic progress, undermine their confidence and self-esteem, and perpetuate cycles of punitive discipline and involvement with the criminal justice system state Skiba et al. (2011). In Kiera's case, the trauma and stigma associated with her arrest and expulsion likely had lasting effects on her educational and personal development. Kiera Wilmot's experience serves as a poignant example of the lived reality of racial bias in school discipline. Her story demonstrates the urgent need for reforms to address systemic inequities in education, including the adoption of restorative justice practices, cultural competency training for educators, and policies that promote equity and fairness in disciplinary decisions.

Eurocentric Curriculum

Ladson-Billings (1995) posits that systemic racism in education is also reflected in the dominance of Eurocentric curriculum and pedagogy that marginalize the histories, cultures, and contributions of BIPOC individuals. The curriculum often prioritizes white perspectives and narratives while neglecting or misre-presenting the experiences of marginalized commu-nities, reinforcing stereotypes and undermining the self-esteem and academic performance of BIPOC students asserts Howard (2018). Nieto (2000) sur-mises this lack of cultural relevance and representation in the curriculum contributes to alienation, disengage-ment and underachievement among BIPOC students.

According to Giroux's (1992) research, the roots of Eurocentric curriculum in education can be traced back to colonialism and imperialism, where European powers imposed their cultural, social, and educational systems on colonized peoples. This legacy of colonial education has contributed to the erasure of Indigenous knowledge systems, languages, and histories, perpe-tuating a narrative of Eurocentrism as the norm and center of knowledge states Smith (1999).

Today, Eurocentric curriculum remains prevalent in many educational institutions, privileging European perspectives and as a bi-product marginalizing the histories, cultures, and contributions of non-European and Indigenous peoples found Banks (1993). This perpetuates a Eurocentric worldview that reinforces racial hierarchies and stereotypes, while excluding diverse voices and experiences from the educational discourse states Sleeter (1993).

The impacts of Eurocentric curriculum on margina-lized communities are profound and multifaceted. Students from non-dominant racial and cultural backgrounds may experience cultural dissonance (a sense of discord, disharmony, confusion, or conflict experienced by people in the midst of change in their cultural environment) and alienation when their identities and experiences are not represented in the curriculum, leading to disengagement and low academic achievement, according to Ladson-Billings (1995).

Sleeter (1993) believes Eurocentric curriculum often perpetuates stereotypes and biases about non-dominant racial and cultural groups, reinforcing negative perceptions and limiting opportunities for students to develop critical consciousness. The imposition of Eurocentric curriculum reflects a colonial legacy that prioritizes Western knowledge systems while erasing Indigenous knowledge, languages, and ways of knowing posits Smith (1999).

An example of the impacts of a Eurocentric curriculum in education can be seen through the experiences of Indigenous students in many Western countries, including the United States, Canada, Australia, and New Zealand. Indigenous students often encounter curricula that prioritize Eurocentric perspectives, histories, and worldviews, while marginalizing or omitting Indigenous knowledge, cultures, and contributions.

For instance, in the United States, Native American students may attend schools where the curriculum largely ignores or misrepresents Indigenous histories, cultures, and contemporary experiences. Instead, they are taught from textbooks and materials that predominantly focus on European colonization, American exceptionalism, and Western achievements, while glossing over the legacies of settler colonialism, genocide, and cultural erasure experienced by Indigenous peoples (Brayboy & Castagno, 2008).

This Eurocentric curriculum not only fails to reflect the lived experiences of Indigenous students but also perpetuates stereotypes, biases, and a sense of cultural invisibility and inferiority. It reinforces the notion that Indigenous cultures and knowledge are less valuable or relevant than Eurocentric perspectives, contributing to feelings of alienation, disengagement, and low self-esteem among Indigenous students (Szasz & Carpenter, 2012).

Furthermore, the absence of Indigenous perspectives and histories in the curriculum deprives all students of a comprehensive understanding of the diverse cultures, histories, and contributions of Indigenous peoples. It perpetuates ignorance, misconceptions, and stereotypes about Indigenous communities, hindering efforts towards reconciliation, mutual understanding, and respect (Battiste, 2013).

In Canada, for example, the Truth and Reconciliation Commission (TRC) highlighted the need for transformative changes to the education system to incorporate Indigenous perspectives, histories, and knowledge. The TRC called for the development of curricula that reflect the experiences and contributions of Indigenous peoples, promote cultural competency and understanding, and support Indigenous students' identities and well-being (Truth and Reconciliation Commission of Canada, 2015). The experiences of Indigenous students highlight the detrimental impacts of a Eurocentric curriculum in education. Addressing these impacts requires systemic changes to the curriculum that center Indigenous perspectives, histories, and knowledge, promote cultural diversity and inclusivity, and support the holistic well-being of Indigenous students.

Limited Access to Higher Education

Systemic racism in education also affects access to higher education for students of color, particularly Black and Latinx students asserts Bowen et al. (2009). Despite efforts to increase diversity and inclusion in higher education, racial gaps in college enrollment, persistence, and completion persist, reflecting broader disparities in K-12 education according to Hurtado et al's (2012) research. Factors such as inadequate preparation, lack of financial aid, and institutional barriers continue to hinder the educational attainment and social mobility of BIPOC students posits Swail et al. (2005).

The historical roots of limited access to higher education for marginalized communities can be traced back to institutionalized racism, segregation, and discriminatory practices in education. Throughout history, racial segregation in schools, unequal funding, and exclusionary admission policies have systematically denied opportunities for Blacks/African Americans, Latinx, Indigenous peoples, and other marginalized groups to pursue higher education Orfield and Eaton's (1996) research demonstrates.

Despite legal advances such as desegregation and affirmative action, racial disparities persist in higher education access and attainment. Structural barriers, such as unequal K-12 education, standardized testing requirements, financial barriers, and lack of representation in academia, contribute to limited access to higher education for marginalized communities according to the findings of Harper and Gasman (2008).

Limited access to higher education perpetuates educational inequities and widens the achievement gap between racial and ethnic groups, reinforcing systemic racism and social stratification state Bowen and Bok (1998). Further, higher education is often seen as a pathway to socioeconomic mobility and opportunity. However, limited access to higher education restricts economic advancement and perpetuates poverty cycles within marginalized communities claim Baum and Steele (2010). Moreover, Perez Huber and Solorzano (2015) argue limited access to higher education contributes to underrepresentation of marginalized groups in leadership positions within academia, government, and other sectors, perpetuating power imbalances and exclusionary practices.

An example of the impacts of limited access to higher education can be seen through the lived experiences of individuals from low-income or marginalized communities who face barriers to pursuing post-secondary education due to financial constraints, lack of educational resources, and systemic inequities.

For instance, consider the experience of Maria, a first-generation college student from a low-income neighborhood. Despite excelling academically in high school, Maria faced numerous challenges in accessing higher education. Her family could not afford the high cost of tuition, textbooks, and other expenses associated with attending college. Additionally, her high school lacked resources such as college counseling and SAT preparation courses, which are often available in more affluent school districts.

As a result, Maria was forced to navigate the complex college admissions process largely on her own, without access to guidance or support from knowledgeable mentors. She struggled to secure financial aid and scholarships to cover the cost of tuition, and she faced limited options for affordable higher education institutions within commuting distance of her home. Despite her determination and hard work, Maria's dreams of attending college were thwarted by systemic barriers beyond her control.

Without the financial resources, educational support, and opportunities afforded to more privileged students, individuals like Maria are disproportionately excluded from the benefits of higher education, perpetuating cycles of poverty and inequality states Goldrick-Rab (2016).

Furthermore, the lack of diversity and representation in higher education institutions further compounds the challenges faced by marginalized students. Students from underrepresented backgrounds may struggle to find a sense of belonging and support on predominantly white campuses, leading to feelings of isolation and alienation contend Harper and Hurtado (2007).

In the long term, limited access to higher education perpetuates social and economic disparities, restricting opportunities for upward mobility and exacerbating existing inequalities in society assert Chetty et al. (2017). Without intervention to address systemic barriers and expand access to higher education for all individuals, the cycle of disadvantage will persist, depriving countless talented and motivated individuals of the opportunity to reach their full potential. Maria's experience illustrates the far-reaching impacts of limited access to higher education on individuals from marginalized communities.

Perpetuation of Socioeconomic Inequality

Systemic racism in education perpetuates socio-economic inequality and limits the opportunities for upward mobility among BIPOC communities claim Reardon and Portilla (2016). By depriving students of color of quality education and resources, the education system reinforces existing disparities in income, wealth, and access to opportunity, exacerbating cycles of poverty and marginalization assert Darity et al. (2006). Moreover, Irizarry (2016) posits that the lack of diversity in educational leadership and policymaking further perpetuates systemic racism and undermines efforts to promote equity and inclusion in education.

The racial disparities that persist in education contribute to socioeconomic inequality. Reardon and Owens' (2014) research demonstrates structural barriers such as unequal funding for schools, disparities in resources and opportunities, and racial bias in disciplinary practices perpetuate socioeconomic disparities and limit access to quality education for marginalized communities.

Marginalized communities often have limited access to quality education due to disparities in school funding, resources, and opportunities, perpetuating socioeconomic inequality and limiting social mobility affirm Duncan and Murnane (2011). Systemic racism in education contributes to widening achievement gaps between racial and ethnic groups, reinforcing socio-economic disparities and perpetuating cycles of poverty and disadvantage suggests Reardon (2011). Limited access to quality education restricts opportunities for higher education and employment, further exacerbating socioeconomic inequality and hindering economic mobility for marginalized communities according to Carnevale et al. (2015).

An example of the impacts of socioeconomic inequality in education can be illustrated through the lived experiences of students attending under-resourced public schools in low-income neighborhoods, where they face systemic barriers to academic achievement and educational opportunities.

Consider the case of Jamal, a student growing up in a disadvantaged urban area. Jamal attends a public school where resources are scarce, class sizes are large, and the infrastructure is deteriorating. The school lacks access to modern technology, up-to-date textbooks, and extracurricular activities that are commonplace in more affluent school districts. As a result, Jamal's educational experience is characterized by overcrowded classrooms, limited instructional support, and inadequate facilities.

Furthermore, Jamal's family struggles to make ends meet, and he often faces challenges outside of school, such as housing instability, food insecurity, and limited access to healthcare. These socioeconomic stressors compound the barriers to academic success, as Jamal grapples with the effects of poverty and inequality on his ability to focus on his studies and pursue his educational goals.

Despite his resilience and determination, Jamal's opportunities for academic advancement are constrained by the systemic inequities that pervade his educational environment. Without access to the resources, support, and opportunities afforded to more privileged students, Jamal's prospects for college admission, career readiness, and upward mobility are limited assert Reardon (2011). These disparities perpetuate cycles of poverty and disadvantage, limiting opportunities for economic advancement and perpetuating intergenerational inequalities contend Duncan and Murnane (2014).

Furthermore, the unequal distribution of educational resources and opportunities reinforces existing disparities in society, perpetuating patterns of social stratification and exacerbating inequalities along racial, ethnic, and socioeconomic lines (Reardon, 2011). Without concerted efforts to address socioeconomic inequality in education, the promise of equal opportunity and social mobility remains elusive for millions of students like Jamal who are trapped in the cycle of poverty and disadvantage. Jamal's experience highlights the profound impacts of socioeconomic inequality in education on individual students, families, and communities.

Investing in early childhood education programs, such as universal pre-kindergarten and early intervention services, can mitigate the effects of systemic racism and socioeconomic inequality on educational outcomes insist Heckman et al. (2010). Further, recruiting and retaining a diverse teaching workforce and providing training in cultural competence can promote equity and inclusivity in education and improve outcomes for marginalized students purport Jackson and Bruegmann (2009).

Moreover, engaging and empowering marginalized communities in the decision-making process and investing in community-led initiatives can promote social cohesion, resilience, and collective action to address systemic racism and socioeconomic inequality in education suggests Warren and Mapp's (2011) research. Systemic racism in education perpetuates socioeconomic inequality by limiting access to quality education and widening achievement gaps between racial and ethnic groups.

Strategies for Addressing
Systemic Racism in Education

Addressing the aforementioned education disparities within the five subcategories requires a concerted effort to dismantle the structural barriers and inequitable practices that perpetuate systemic racism in education. By implementing targeted interventions aimed at promoting equity, inclusivity, and opportunity for all students, policymakers, educators, and community stakeholders can work towards creating a more just and equitable education system that fosters the success of all learners, regardless of race or socioeconomic status. Some strategies for addressing systemic racism in education (in addition to those briefly covered as various points within the chapter) include the following.

1. Ensuring equitable funding and resources for all schools, regardless of the racial or socioeconomic composition of their student body, is essential for addressing systemic racism in education asserts Siddle-Walker (1996). Orfield and Eaton (1996) concur, declaring equitable funding must be ensured for K-12 schools and higher education institutions serving marginalized communities to reduce disparities in resources and opportunities. This includes allocating additional resources to schools serving high-needs students, reducing reliance on property taxes for school funding, and implementing weighted funding formulas that account for student demographics and needs according to Kober and Rentner (2011). Furthermore, Baum and Steele (2010) stipulate increasing access to financial aid, scholarships, and other forms of financial assistance can alleviate the burden of college affordability and facilitate access to higher education for low-income and marginalized students.

2. Promoting culturally relevant curriculum and pedagogy that reflect the diversity of students' backgrounds and experiences is critical for addressing systemic racism in education posits Gay (2010). This includes integrating diverse perspectives, histories, and voices into the curriculum, providing opportunities for students to explore their identities and cultural heritage, and fostering critical consciousness and social awareness suggests Ladson-Billings (2014).

Furthermore, Ladson-Billings (1995) suggests implementation of culturally relevant pedagogies to integrate students' cultural backgrounds, experiences, and perspectives into the curriculum fosters a sense of belonging and promotes academic success. Also, Camangian (2012) believes introducing critical ethnic studies frameworks is vital to challenge Eurocentric curriculum by centering the histories, experiences, and resistance of marginalized racial and ethnic groups, disrupting dominant narratives and promoting social justice.

3. Implementing restorative justice practices and alternatives to traditional disciplinary measures can help reduce racial disparities in school discipline and promote positive school climate and student engagement affirms Gregory et al. (2016). Restorative justice approaches focus on repairing harm, building relationships, and addressing the underlying causes of conflict and misbehavior, rather than simply punishing students Morrison et al. (2010).

4. Promoting diversity and inclusion in educational leadership and policymaking is essential for addressing systemic racism in education suggest Parker et al. (2013). This includes recruiting and retaining educators and administrators from diverse racial and cultural backgrounds, providing professional development on issues of equity and social justice, and involving students, families, and communities in

decision-making processes believes Grogan and Shakeshaft (2011).

Additionally, Bowen and Bok (1998) maintain affirmative action policies that prioritize diversity and inclusion in college admissions can increase access to higher education for underrepresented racial and ethnic groups. However, the U.S. Supreme Court ended affirmative action in higher education in June 2023, stating its practice violates Title VI of the Civil Rights Act of 1964 and the Equal Protection Clause of the Fourteenth Amendment reports Austin (2023).

In conclusion, systemic racism in education has profound and far-reaching impacts on students, educators, and communities of color. By perpetuating disparities in funding, resources, discipline, curriculum, and access to higher education, the education system reinforces racial inequalities and limits opportunities for upward mobility. Addressing systemic racism in education requires a comprehensive and intersectional approach that addresses the root causes of racial disparities and promotes equity and social justice. By investing in equitable funding, culturally relevant curriculum and pedagogy, restorative justice practices, and diverse and inclusive leadership, we can work towards creating a more just and equitable education system for all.

4
Systemic Racism in Healthcare

4
The Impacts of Systemic Racism on Healthcare

Within the healthcare system, systemic racism manifests in various ways, leading to disparities in access to care, quality of care, and health outcomes for Black, Indigenous, and people of color (BIPOC) communities assert Bailey et al. (2017). These disparities contribute to significant health inequities, exacerbating the burden of disease and mortality rates among marginalized populations according to Williams and Mohammed's (2009) research. In this chapter, the effects of systemic racism on healthcare are examined and methods are proposed to address these disparities.

Historical Context
Systemic racism has deep roots in the history of healthcare in the United States, with marginalized communities, particularly BIPOC, experiencing discrimination and mistreatment within the healthcare system. One of the most infamous examples of systemic racism in healthcare is the Tuskegee Syphilis Study, conducted by the United States Public Health Service from 1932 to 1972. In this study, researchers withheld treatment from hundreds of Black men with syphilis, denying them access to life-saving medical care and allowing the disease to progress untreated according to Jones et al's (2008) research. Washington's (2006) research concludes this egregious violation of medical ethics demonstrated the disregard for the health and well-being of Black individuals within the healthcare system from that era to the present one.

Additionally, the forced sterilization of Indigenous women and women of color throughout the 20th century is another example of systemic racism in healthcare. Under state-sponsored eugenics pro-grams, Indigenous women and women of color were subjected to coerced sterilization procedures without their informed consent, further perpetuating repro-ductive injustices and violating their bodily autonomy claims Stern (2005).

These historical injustices have had lasting effects on trust in the healthcare system among BIPOC communities, contributing to disparities in health-seeking behaviors and health outcomes. The legacy of medical exploitation and abuse continues to shape perceptions of healthcare among marginalized popu-lations, highlighting the importance of addressing systemic racism in healthcare to promote health equity and justice for all.

Access to Healthcare

Access to healthcare is a fundamental determinant of health, yet systemic racism perpetuates significant disparities in access to care, particularly for margi-nalized communities such as Black, Indigenous, and people of color (BIPOC). Systemic racism manifests in various forms, including structural barriers, discrimi-natory practices, and unequal distribution of resources, all of which contribute to inequities in access to healthcare services.

Structural Barriers

Structural barriers, such as lack of health insu-rance, transportation issues, and geographic dispa-rities in healthcare infrastructure, disproportionately affect BIPOC communities and hinder their access to healthcare services attest Bailey et al. (2017). Accor-ding to the U.S. Census Bureau, BIPOC individuals are more likely to be uninsured compared to their white counterparts, with Latinx and Black individuals experi-encing the highest rates of uninsurance according to

Artiga et al. (2016). Without health insurance coverage, individuals may delay seeking medical care or forego preventive services due to financial constraints, leading to worsened health outcomes over time.

Transportation barriers also pose significant challenges to accessing healthcare, particularly for individuals living in rural or low-income areas with limited public transportation options. BIPOC communities are more likely to reside in neighborhoods with inadequate access to healthcare facilities, resulting in longer travel times and difficulties accessing timely medical care suggests Artiga et al. (2016). These geographic disparities exacerbate existing health inequities and contribute to disparities in health outcomes among BIPOC populations.

Discriminatory Practices

Discriminatory practices within the healthcare system further compound access barriers for BIPOC individuals. FitzGerald and Hurst's (2017) research has documented instances of racial bias and discrimination by healthcare providers, resulting in differential treatment and disparities in care. Implicit biases held by healthcare professionals may influence clinical decision-making and patient interactions, leading to disparities in diagnosis, treatment, and referrals for BIPOC patients according to Green et al's (2007) research. Studies by Hoffman et al. (2016) have shown that Black patients are less likely to receive appropriate pain management compared to white patients, high-lighting the impact of racial bias on access to quality care.

Unequal Distribution of Resources

The unequal distribution of healthcare resources, including medical facilities, equipment, and healthcare providers, contributes to disparities in access to care for BIPOC communities. Research has documented disparities in the availability of primary care providers and specialty services in predominantly BIPOC neighborhoods, leading to limited access to comprehensive care states the Agency for Healthcare Research and Quality (2018). Additionally, BIPOC communities are more likely to experience shortages of healthcare professionals, including physicians, nurses, and mental health providers, further exacerbating access barriers assert Bailey et al. (2017).

An example of the impacts of systemic racism on access to healthcare can be seen through the lived experiences of Black Americans who face barriers to obtaining timely and quality medical care due to racial discrimination and structural inequities within the healthcare system.

Consider the case of Sarah, a Black woman who experiences symptoms of chest pain and shortness of breath. Concerned about her health, Sarah seeks medical attention at a local hospital emergency room. However, upon arrival, she is met with skepticism and dismissive attitudes from healthcare providers who downplay her symptoms and attribute them to anxiety or stress, rather than conducting a thorough evaluation and diagnostic workup.

Despite her insistence on the severity of her symptoms, Sarah's concerns are not taken seriously, and she is ultimately discharged from the hospital without receiving appropriate treatment or follow-up care. As a result, Sarah's condition worsens over time, and she experiences significant delays in receiving the medical attention she urgently needs.

Sarah's experience is not unique and reflects broader patterns of racial bias and discrimination within the healthcare system. Research has consistently shown that Black patients are more likely to encounter barriers to accessing healthcare services, including longer wait times, lower rates of insurance coverage, and fewer options for medical treatment attest Burgess et al. (2008).

The impacts of systemic racism on access to healthcare extend beyond individual experiences like Sarah's to shape broader patterns of health inequality and disparities in society. Structural barriers such as residential segregation, limited access to healthcare facilities, and unequal distribution of resources perpetuate inequities in healthcare access and quality for Black communities assert Baicker et al. (2017). Sarah's experience demonstrates the urgent need to address systemic racism within the healthcare system and ensure equitable access to healthcare for all individuals, regardless of their race or ethnicity.

Quality of Care

The effects of systemic racism manifest in various ways within the healthcare system, contributing to disparities in care delivery, patient outcomes, and patient experiences.

Healthcare Disparities

Systemic racism perpetuates healthcare disparities that result in differential access to and utilization of healthcare services among BIPOC populations. Williams and Wyatt's (2015) research has consistently demonstrated that BIPOC individuals experience lower quality of care across a range of healthcare settings, including primary care, specialty care, and hospital services. These disparities are multifaceted and encompass various aspects of care, including preventive services, diagnostic accuracy, treatment options, and patient-provider communication assert Bailey et al. (2017).

For example, studies have shown that BIPOC patients are less likely to receive recommended preventive screenings and vaccinations compared to their white counterparts, leading to delays in diagnosis and treatment of preventable diseases posit the Agency for Healthcare Research and Quality (2018).

Additionally, BIPOC patients are more likely to experience diagnostic delays and misdiagnoses, resulting in poorer health outcomes and increased mortality rates according to Howell et al's (2016) research.

Provider Bias and Discrimination

Provider bias and discrimination also contribute to disparities in quality of care experienced by BIPOC patients. FitzGerald and Hurst's (2017) research has documented instances of racial bias and stereotyping among healthcare providers, which can influence clinical decision-making and patient interactions. Implicit biases held by healthcare professionals may result in differential treatment recommendations, medication prescribing practices, and referrals for BIPOC patients, leading to disparities in care quality according to Green et al. (2007).

Furthermore, discriminatory practices within the healthcare system, such as patient profiling, racial profiling, and unequal treatment based on race or ethnicity, contribute to disparities in quality of care suggest Williams and Wyatt (2015). BIPOC patients are more likely to report experiences of discrimination and mistreatment within healthcare settings, which can undermine trust in the healthcare system and deter individuals from seeking timely medical care as shown in Gamble et al's (2018) findings.

Cultural Competence and Communication

Cultural competence and effective communication are essential components of high-quality healthcare delivery, yet systemic racism undermines these principles within the healthcare system. BIPOC patients often encounter cultural and linguistic barriers when interacting with healthcare providers, resulting in miscommunication, misunderstandings, and suboptimal care experiences state Betancourt et al. (2003).

Additionally, healthcare providers may lack awareness of the cultural values, beliefs, and practices of
BIPOC communities, leading to insensitive or inappro-
priate care delivery stipulate Brach and Fraser (2000).
Culturally competent care requires healthcare providers to acknowledge and respect the cultural diversity
of their patient population, adapt their communication
style and care approach accordingly, and actively
engage with patients as partners in care decision-
making insist Betancourt et al. (2003).

Maternal and Infant Health Disparities

Systemic racism plays a significant role in
perpetuating maternal and infant health disparities,
contributing to adverse outcomes for BIPOC mothers
and infants. These disparities are multifaceted and
encompass various aspects of the maternal and infant
healthcare continuum, including prenatal care, childbirth experiences, postpartum care, and infant health
outcomes.

Prenatal Care Disparities

Wallace et al. (2016) posit that access to prenatal
care is a critical determinant of maternal and infant
health outcomes, yet systemic racism contributes to
disparities in prenatal care utilization among BIPOC
communities. Structural barriers, such as lack of health
insurance, transportation issues, and geographic
disparities in healthcare access, disproportionately
affect BIPOC individuals and hinder their access to
prenatal care services. Additionally, Howell et al's
(2016) research provides evidence of discriminatory
practices within the healthcare system, including racial
bias and stereotyping, that may influence providers'
interactions with BIPOC pregnant individuals, leading
to disparities in the quality and frequency of prenatal
care received.

Childbirth Experiences and Maternal Health Outcomes

Systemic racism also influences childbirth experiences and maternal health outcomes for BIPOC individuals, contributing to disparities in maternal mortality and morbidity. BIPOC mothers are more likely to experience complications during childbirth, including maternal hemorrhage, preeclampsia, and cesarean section deliveries, compared to white mothers found Howell et al. (2016). These disparities are driven by a combination of factors, including structural barriers to care, provider bias and discrimination, and unequal distribution of healthcare resources assert Wallace et al. (2016). BIPOC mothers are also more likely to receive suboptimal care during childbirth, including inadequate pain management and delays in obstetric interventions, which contribute to adverse maternal health outcomes stipulate Howell et al. (2016).

Postpartum Care Disparities

Disparities in postpartum care further exacerbate maternal health inequities for BIPOC individuals. Howell et al's (2016) research found BIPOC mothers are less likely to receive timely postpartum care visits and support services compared to white mothers, leading to disparities in postpartum depression screening, contraceptive counseling, and breast-feeding support. Lack of access to comprehensive postpartum care contributes to worsened maternal health outcomes and increased risks of maternal mortality and morbidity among BIPOC mothers according to Wallace et al. (2016).

Infant Health Outcomes

Systemic racism also impacts infant health outcomes, with BIPOC infants experiencing higher rates of preterm birth, low birth weight, and infant mortality compared to white infants posits Howell et al. (2016). These disparities are influenced by a complex interplay of social determinants of health, including socio-economic status, access to healthcare, and exposure to environmental stressors. BIPOC infants are also more likely to experience inadequate access to pediatric care and early intervention services, further exacerbating health inequities and disparities in infant health outcomes found Wallace et al. (2016).

An example of the impacts of systemic racism on the quality of care in healthcare can be demonstrated through the lived experiences of Black women during childbirth, who often face disparities in the quality of maternal healthcare due to racial bias and discrimination within the healthcare system.

Consider the case of Jasmine, a Black woman who is pregnant with her first child. Throughout her pregnancy, Jasmine receives prenatal care from healthcare providers who dismiss her concerns, minimize her symptoms, and fail to provide adequate support and information about her pregnancy and childbirth options.

When Jasmine goes into labor, she arrives at the hospital seeking assistance and guidance from medical professionals. However, she is met with neglectful and disrespectful treatment from hospital staff who ignore her requests for pain relief, fail to monitor her condition closely, and engage in coercive practices such as unnecessary medical interventions and procedures without her consent.

As a result of the substandard care she receives, Jasmine experiences complications during childbirth that could have been prevented with appropriate medical attention and support. Her experience highlights the pervasive impact of systemic racism on the quality of maternal healthcare for Black women, who are disproportionately at risk of experiencing adverse outcomes during pregnancy and childbirth. Black women are disproportionately affected by maternal mortality and morbidity, with higher rates of pregnancy-related complications, maternal deaths, and adverse birth outcomes compared to white women according to Howell et al's (2016) research. Jasmine's experience underscores the urgent need to address systemic racism within the healthcare system and ensure equitable access to high-quality maternal healthcare for all women, regardless of their race or ethnicity.

Mental Health Disparities

Systemic racism exerts a profound influence on mental health disparities, contributing to inequities in access to care, treatment outcomes, and mental health outcomes for BIPOC individuals. These disparities are multifaceted and encompass various dimensions of mental health, including prevalence rates of mental illness, access to mental health services, and quality of care received.

Prevalence of Mental Illness

Systemic racism contributes to disparities in the prevalence rates of mental illness among BIPOC communities. Sue et al's (2012) research has consistently shown that BIPOC individuals experience higher rates of psychological distress, depression, anxiety, and post-traumatic stress disorder (PTSD) compared to their white counterparts. These disparities are driven by a range of social determinants of health, including experiences of discrimination, socioeconomic disadvantage, exposure to trauma and violence, and cultural factors insist Williams and Mohammed (2009). Systemic racism exacerbates these risk factors and creates additional barriers to mental health and well-being for BIPOC individuals.

Access to Mental Health Services

Access to mental health services is a critical determinant of mental health outcomes, yet systemic racism contributes to disparities in access to care for

BIPOC communities. Structural barriers, such as lack of health insurance, limited availability of culturally competent providers, and geographic disparities in mental health resources, disproportionately affect BIPOC individuals and hinder their access to mental health services posit Sue et al. (2012). Additionally, discriminatory practices within the healthcare system, including racial bias and stereotyping, may influence providers' interactions with BIPOC patients, leading to disparities in the quality and appropriateness of mental health care received according to Watson et al. (2018).

Treatment Outcomes
Systemic racism also influences treatment outcomes for BIPOC individuals receiving mental health care, contributing to disparities in treatment adherence, medication management, and therapeutic outcomes. Sue et al's (2012) research has documented instances of racial bias and discrimination in mental health treatment settings, which can undermine the therapeutic alliance between providers and BIPOC patients and impede treatment progress. BIPOC individuals are also more likely to experience discontinuity of care, treatment delays, and inadequate follow-up care compared to white patients, leading to worsened mental health outcomes over time state Watson et al. (2018).

Mental Health Stigma
Systemic racism perpetuates mental health stigma within BIPOC communities, contributing to under-recognition and underreporting of mental health symptoms and reluctance to seek help for mental health concerns. Cultural beliefs, social norms, and historical experiences of medical mistreatment and exploitation shape attitudes towards mental health and help-seeking behaviors among BIPOC individuals, creating barriers to accessing timely and appropriate

care assert Sue et al. (2012). Additionally, Watson et al. (2018) posit that BIPOC individuals may experience intersectional stigma related to race, ethnicity, gender identity, sexual orientation, and socioeconomic status, further complicating their experiences of mental health stigma and discrimination.

An example of the impacts of systemic racism on mental health disparities in healthcare can be illustrated through the lived experiences of Black individuals who face barriers to accessing culturally competent and equitable mental health services due to racial bias and discrimination within the healthcare system.

Consider the case of Malik, a young Black man who experiences symptoms of depression and anxiety. Despite recognizing the need for mental health support, Malik is hesitant to seek help due to stigma surrounding mental illness within his community and concerns about facing discrimination and mistreatment from healthcare providers.

When Malik finally decides to seek assistance from a mental health professional, he encounters numerous challenges in accessing care. He struggles to find a therapist who understands his cultural background and experiences as a Black man, and he faces long wait times and limited availability of mental health services in his community.

Furthermore, when Malik does receive mental health treatment, he encounters racial bias and discrimination from healthcare providers who lack cultural competence and fail to acknowledge or address the unique stressors and traumas experienced by Black individuals. As a result, Malik feels misunderstood, invalidated, and unsupported in his mental health journey, exacerbating his symptoms and hindering his recovery.

Malik's experience is emblematic of the broader disparities in mental health care faced by Black individuals, who are less likely to receive appropriate diagnosis, treatment, and support for mental health conditions compared to their white counterparts according to Williams et al. (2007). Research has consistently shown that Black individuals experience higher rates of psychological distress, depression, and suicide compared to white individuals, yet they are less likely to receive mental health services and are more likely to receive lower-quality care when they do seek help asserts Sue et al. (2009).

These disparities reflect systemic barriers to mental health care access and quality, including structural racism, socioeconomic inequality, and cultural insensitivity within the healthcare system contends Whaley (2001). Black individuals often face limited access to mental health services, lack of insurance coverage, and geographic barriers to care, as well as mistrust of healthcare providers and stigma surrounding mental illness within their communities claims Snowden (2001).

Malik's experience demonstrates the urgent need to address systemic racism within the mental healthcare system and ensure equitable access to culturally competent and high-quality mental health services for Black individuals and other marginalized communities.

Systemic racism perpetuates significant disparities in access to healthcare, quality of care, maternal and infant health disparities, and mental health disparities. These multifaceted disparities pose barriers to care for BIPOC communities and contribute to health inequities. Specifically, structural barriers, discriminatory practices, and unequal distribution of resources; provider bias and discrimination, and cultural competence and communication; prenatal care disparities, childbirth experiences, maternal health outcomes, postpartum care disparities, and infant health outcomes; prevalence of mental illness, access to mental health services, treatment outcomes, and mental health stigma all contribute to access disparities within the healthcare system.

Addressing Healthcare Disparities

Six specific measures can be implemented to dismantle the effects of racial discrimination in healthcare.

Adequate Access to Healthcare
Access to healthcare requires comprehensive strategies that address both structural barriers and discriminatory practices within the healthcare system. Policy interventions, such as expanding Medicaid coverage, improving transportation infrastructure, and increasing funding for underserved communities, can help alleviate access barriers for BIPOC populations posit Williams and Wyatt (2015). Additionally, Betancourt et al. (2003) state efforts to promote cultural competence and diversity in the healthcare workforce are essential for ensuring equitable care delivery and addressing disparities in access to quality care.

Promoting Culturally Competent Care
Promoting culturally competent care is essential for addressing healthcare disparities caused by systemic racism. Culturally competent care involves recognizing and respecting the cultural beliefs, values, and practices of diverse patient populations and tailoring care to meet their unique needs state Betancourt et al. (2003). Healthcare providers must undergo training to recognize and address their own biases, understand the cultural context of their patients, and communicate effectively across language and cultural barriers assert Brach and Fraser (2000). By promoting culturally competent care, healthcare organizations can improve patient-provider communication, increase patient satisfaction, and reduce disparities in healthcare delivery posits Cuevas et al. (2016).

Increasing Diversity in the Healthcare Workforce
Increasing diversity in the healthcare workforce is critical for addressing systemic racism in healthcare. Research has shown that racial and ethnic concordance between patients and providers is associated with better communication, higher patient satisfaction, and improved health outcomes insist Saha et al.

(2000). By recruiting and retaining more BIPOC health-care professionals, healthcare organizations can improve cultural competence, reduce implicit biases, and provide better care to diverse patient populations assert Cohen et al. (2002). Efforts to increase diversity should include targeted recruitment initiatives, scholar-ships, mentorship programs, and support for BIPOC students pursuing careers in healthcare state Smedley et al. (2003).

Addressing Social Determinants of Health

Many healthcare disparities stem from social deter-minants of health, such as poverty, housing insecurity, and lack of access to education. Addressing these underlying social factors is essential for improving health outcomes and reducing disparities among BIPOC communities suggest Braveman et al. (2011). Healthcare organizations can collaborate with community-based organizations, government agen-cies, and social service providers to address social determinants of health through initiatives, such as affordable housing programs, job training programs, and access to healthy food options according to Gottlieb et al's research (2016). By addressing social determinants of health, healthcare organizations can address the root causes of health disparities and promote health equity in marginalized communities.

Advocating for Policy Changes

Policy changes at the local, state, and federal levels are needed to dismantle systemic racism in healthcare. This includes implementing anti-discrimi-nation policies, expanding Medicaid coverage, and investing in healthcare infrastructure in underserved communities according to Williams and Wyatt (2015). Additionally, policymakers must address systemic issues such as institutional racism in medical edu-cation, funding disparities for minority-serving institutions, and inequities in research funding posit Gamble et al. (2018). By advocating for policy changes, healthcare organizations can create a more equitable and just healthcare system that serves the needs of all patients.

Engaging with and Empowering Marginalized Communities

Engaging with and empowering BIPOC communities to advocate for their healthcare needs is crucial for addressing healthcare disparities caused by systemic racism according to Israel et al. (2003). Healthcare organizations should involve community members in decision-making processes, seek input on healthcare policies and programs, and provide resources and support for community-led initiatives provides Minkler and Wallerstein's research (2008). Jones and Wells (2007) believes by centering the voices and experiences of marginalized communities, healthcare organizations can develop more effective strategies for addressing systemic racism in healthcare.

Systemic racism continues to be a significant barrier to health equity, resulting in disparities in access to care, quality of care, and health outcomes for marginalized communities. Addressing these disparities requires a multi-faceted approach that includes promoting culturally competent care, increasing diversity in the healthcare workforce, addressing social determinants of health, advocating for policy changes, and engaging with and empowering marginalized communities. By taking concerted action to dismantle systemic racism in healthcare, we can work towards a more equitable and just healthcare system that serves the needs of all patients.

5
Systemic Racism in Employment

5
The Impacts of Systemic Racism on Employment

Systemic racism manifests in various forms within society, with one of its most significant impacts being on employment opportunities for BIPOC individuals. Despite advancements in civil rights and diversity initiatives, racial disparities persist in the workforce, resulting in structural barriers (unequal access) to employment; wage disparities and economic inequality; occupational segregation and limited career advancement opportunities; and psychological and emotional impact. This chapter will explore the multi-faceted impacts of systemic racism on employment, drawing on empirical research and scholarly literature to illuminate the pervasive nature of racial discrimination in the workplace.

Structural Barriers (Unequal Access)

Structural barriers rooted in historical injustices and institutionalized discrimination continue to hinder the equal access and advancement of racial minorities in the workforce effectuated by discriminatory hiring practices, occupational segregation, educational disparities, and lack of access to resources and networks.

Discriminatory Hiring Practices

One of the most pervasive structural barriers to employment faced by BIPOC communities is discriminatory hiring practices. Despite legal protections against discrimination, studies by Pager et al. (2009) have consistently found evidence of racial bias in hiring processes, wherein employers favor white applicants over equally qualified candidates of color. Discrimination occurs at various stages of the hiring process, from resume screening and job interviews to promotion decisions, leading to unequal employment opportunities for racial minorities.

> An example of discriminatory hiring practices can be seen through the lived experience of Robert, an African American job applicant who faces discrimination during the hiring process.
>
> Robert, a highly qualified candidate with years of experience in his field, applies for a managerial position at a prestigious company. He submits his resume, completes the initial screening process, and is invited for an interview. During the interview, Robert impresses the hiring panel with his knowledge, skills, and professional demeanor.
>
> Despite his qualifications, Robert notices subtle signs of bias and discrimination during the interview. The hiring panel members seem less engaged and attentive compared to other candidates. They ask Robert probing questions about his qualifications and experience, questioning whether he is truly qualified for the position.
>
> As the interview progresses, Robert becomes increasingly aware of the racial dynamics at play. He notices that the hiring panel is predominantly white, with no representation from diverse backgrounds. He also observes microaggressions and biased assumptions about his abilities based on his race.
>
> After the interview, Robert receives a polite rejection email from the company, stating that they have decided to move forward with another candidate who they believe is a better fit for the position. Despite his qualifications and strong performance during the interview, Robert suspects that his race played a significant role in the hiring decision.
>
> This experience highlights the pervasive nature of discriminatory hiring practices that persist in many workplaces. Despite efforts to promote diversity and inclusion, implicit bias and systemic racism continue to influence hiring decisions, disadvantaging qualified candidates from marginalized backgrounds posit Pager et al. (2009).

Research has shown that African American job applicants face discrimination at various stages of the hiring process, including resume screening, job interviews, and job offers assert Bertrand and Mullainathan (2004). Discriminatory hiring practices not only perpetuate racial disparities in employment but also contribute to economic inequality and social injustice. Robert's experience exemplifies the lived reality of discriminatory hiring practices faced by many individuals from marginalized communities.

Occupational Segregation

Another consequence of structural racism in employment is occupational segregation, wherein BIPOC individuals are disproportionately concentrated in low-paying and low-status occupations with limited opportunities for advancement asserts Wilson (2009). This segregation is perpetuated by various factors, including historical patterns of discrimination, lack of access to quality education and training, and institutionalized bias within hiring and promotion processes. As a result, racial minorities face restricted mobility within the labor market, hindering their ability to secure stable and well-paying jobs.

An example of occupational segregation can be illustrated through the lived experience of Esmeralda, a Latina who faces barriers to advancement and opportunities for career growth in her workplace due to systemic biases and occupational segregation.

Esmeralda works in a large corporate organization where she is one of the few women of color in a managerial role. Despite her qualifications and performance, Esmeralda notices that she is consistently overlooked for promotions and leadership opportunities compared to her white male colleagues.

In meetings and decision-making processes, Esmeralda often finds herself sidelined or ignored, while her male counterparts receive more recognition and opportunities for career advancement. She notices a pattern of occupational segregation within her organization, with women and people of color disproportionately represented in lower-paying and lower-status positions.

Despite her efforts to advocate for herself and demonstrate her capabilities, Esmeralda faces systemic barriers to advancement, including implicit bias, stereotypes, and lack of representation in leadership positions. She struggles to break through the glass ceiling and overcome the structural inequalities that perpetuate occupational segregation in her workplace.

Esmeralda's experience is emblematic of the broader patterns of occupational segregation that persist in many industries and workplaces. Research has shown that women, particularly women of color, are over-represented in low-wage and low-status occupations and under-represented in leadership roles and higher-paying positions according to Reskin and McBrier's (2000) research.

Occupational segregation contributes to gender and racial disparities in wages, job opportunities, and career advancement, perpetuating inequality and limiting economic mobility for marginalized groups contends Tomaskovic-Devey et al. (2006). Despite efforts to promote diversity and inclusion, occupational segregation remains a pervasive and entrenched issue in the labor market.

Esmeralda's experience highlights the lived reality of occupational segregation faced by many women and people of color in the workforce.

Educational Disparities

Educational disparities represent another structural barrier to employment for racial minorities, as unequal access to quality education limits their opportunities for economic advancement. Orfield and Lee (2005) posit that due to factors such as residential segregation, underfunded schools, and racial discrimination within educational systems, racial minorities are more likely to attend poorly resourced schools and receive lower-quality education compared to their white counterparts. This educational disadvantage translates into limited employment prospects and reduced earning potential for racial minorities, perpetuating cycles of intergenerational poverty and inequality.

Lack of Access to Resources and Networks

BIPOC individuals also face barriers to employment stemming from their limited access to resources and social networks that facilitate job acquisition and career advancement. Fernandez and Castilla's (2020) research suggests discrimination and exclusion from professional networks and social circles often impede the ability of racial minorities to access job opportunities, mentorship programs, and career development initiatives. As a result, they are disproportionately underrepresented in high-paying professions and leadership positions, further entrenching patterns of economic inequality and exclusion.

Wage Disparities and Economic Inequality

Despite legal protections against discrimination, BIPOC communities continue to experience unequal access to employment opportunities and disparities in wages, contributing to the persistence of racial economic inequality.

Wage Disparities and Discriminatory Practices

One of the most significant manifestations of systemic racism in employment is wage disparities, wherein BIPOC individuals are systematically paid less than their white counterparts for comparable work according to Altonji and Blank (1999). Despite advancements in civil rights legislation, studies have consistently found evidence of racial bias in wage-setting processes, wherein racial minorities are under-valued and undercompensated relative to their skills and qualifications posits Pager and Shepherd (2008). Discriminatory practices such as wage theft, unequal pay for equal work, and exclusion from high-paying professions contribute to the perpetuation of racial wage gaps and economic inequality.

An example of wage disparities can be seen through the lived experience of Michael and Maria, two employees working in the same company with similar qualifications and experience, but who receive different wages due to gender and racial biases.

Michael, a white male employee, and Maria, a Latina employee, both work as software engineers in a technology company. They have comparable educational backgrounds, skills, and years of experience in the field. However, when they compare their salaries, they discover a significant wage gap between them.

Despite performing similar job duties and contributing equally to the success of the company, Michael earns a higher salary than Maria. When they inquire about the wage disparity, they are told that it is based on factors such as negotiation skills, performance evaluations, and market demand. However, they suspect that gender and racial biases may also play a role in the wage gap.

Maria feels frustrated and undervalued, knowing she is paid less than her male counterpart for doing the same work. She realizes wage disparities based on gender and race are not only unfair but also perpetuate systemic inequalities in the workplace.

Michael acknowledges his privilege as a white male and recognizes the need to advocate for pay equity and fairness in the workplace. He joins Maria in raising awareness about the wage gap and advocating for policy changes to address gender and racial disparities in compensation.

Their experience highlights the pervasive nature of wage disparities based on gender and race in many industries and workplaces. Research has consistently shown that women and people of color are paid less than their white male counterparts, even when they have similar qualifications and perform the same job duties attest Blau and Kahn (2017).

Wage disparities contribute to economic inequality and perpetuate systemic biases and discrimination in the labor market. Despite efforts to promote pay equity and transparency, wage gaps persist, reflecting broader patterns of gender and racial inequality in society according to Altonji and Blank (1999). Michael and Maria's experience exemplifies the lived reality of wage disparities based on gender and race in the workforce.

Limited Advancement Opportunities

Research indicates that BIPOC individuals face disproportionate challenges in accessing and progressing within the workforce. Studies conducted by Reskin and McBrier (2000) and Tomaskovic-Devey et al. (2006) have shown that they are underrepresented in leadership positions and higher-paying roles compared to their white counterparts. This underrepresentation is often attributed to systemic biases in hiring, promotion, and organizational culture, which disadvantage BIPOC employees and perpetuate disparities in career advancement.

Additionally, BIPOC employees frequently encounter barriers to advancement, such as implicit bias, discrimination, and lack of mentorship and sponsorship opportunities state Pager et al. (2009) and Bertrand and Mullainathan (2004). These barriers can impede their ability to access leadership roles, receive promotions, and develop the skills and networks necessary for career progression. As a result, BIPOC employees may experience stagnation in their careers and limited opportunities for professional development and upward mobility.

> An example of a lived experience can be seen through Joseph, an African American employee, who has been working at a multinational corporation for several years. Despite his dedication, hard work, and excellent performance evaluations, Joseph finds himself continually passed over for promotions and leadership opportunities. Joseph notices that many of his white colleagues with similar qualifications and experience are consistently chosen for advancement, while he remains stuck in his current position.
>
> Joseph's experience is emblematic of the limited advancement opportunities faced by BIPOC employees in the workplace. Joseph observes a lack of diversity in the company's leadership ranks, with predominantly white executives making decisions about promotions and career development. Despite his qualifications and aspirations for advancement, Joseph feels that he is not given the same opportunities for career growth as his white colleagues. He faces barriers such as implicit bias, discrimination, and lack of mentorship and sponsorship, which hinder his ability to progress within the organization.
>
> Joseph's experience highlights the intersectional nature of limited advancement opportunities, where race, ethnicity, and other identities intersect to create barriers to career advancement. Despite his skills and qualifications, Joseph's identity as an African American man contributes to his marginalization within the workplace and limits his opportunities for professional growth.

Educational Disparities and Skill Mismatches

Orfield and Lee (2005) report educational disparities represent another structural barrier to economic equality, as racial minorities are disproportionately underrepresented in higher education and face limited access to quality educational opportunities. As a result, they are more likely to possess lower levels of educational attainment and skills compared to their white counterparts, leading to skill mismatches and diminished earning potential in the labor market state Kochhar et al. (2016). Educational differentials contribute to the perpetuation of wage disparities and economic inequality, further entrenching patterns of economic disadvantage among racial minorities.

Occupational Segregation and Limited Career Advancement

Occupational segregation and limited career advancement represent significant challenges faced by racial minorities in the labor market, perpetuating systemic racism and contributing to economic inequality.

Patterns of Occupational Segregation

Reskin and Roos (1990) consider occupational segregation as the unequal distribution of workers across occupations based on factors such as race, ethnicity, gender, and socioeconomic status. Studies performed by Pager et al. (2009) have consistently found evidence of racial disparities in occupational attainment, with BIPOC individuals disproportionately represented in low-paying and low-status occupations relative to their white counterparts. This segregation is perpetuated by various factors, including historical patterns of discrimination, lack of access to quality education and training, and institutionalized bias within hiring and promotion processes.

Consequences of Occupational Segregation

Occupational segregation has far-reaching consequences for racial minorities, limiting their access to economic opportunities and career advancement. Racial minorities employed in segregated occupations often face lower wages, reduced benefits, and limited opportunities for skill development and upward mobility asserts Wilson (2009). Moreover, Fernandez and Castilla's (2020) research revealed segregation isolates racial minorities from professional networks and mentorship opportunities, hindering their ability to access job opportunities and advance in their careers. As a result, they are disproportionately underrepresented in high-paying professions and leadership positions, perpetuating cycles of economic inequality and exclusion.

Institutional and Structural Barriers

Structural barriers within organizations and institutions further exacerbate occupational segregation and limit career advancement opportunities for BIPOC communities. Discriminatory hiring and promotion practices, lack of diversity initiatives, and unequal access to resources and networks all contribute to the perpetuation of racial disparities in the workforce according to Pager and Shepherd's (2008) research. Moreover, racial biases and stereotypes often inform decision-making processes, leading to the marginalization and exclusion of racial minorities from opportunities for advancement and professional development.

Psychological and Emotional Impact

Systemic racism in employment not only perpetuates economic disparities but also inflicts profound psychological and emotional harm on racial minorities.

Psychological Toll of Racial Discrimination

Racial discrimination in employment takes a significant toll on the psychological well-being of racial minorities, leading to increased levels of stress, anxiety, and depression confirms Williams and Mohammed (2009).

Bor et al's (2018) studies have shown that experiences of discrimination in the workplace are associated with adverse mental health outcomes, including symptoms of post-traumatic stress disorder and decreased self-esteem. The constant threat of discrimination and microaggressions creates a hostile work environment that undermines the mental health and well-being of racial minorities, contributing to feelings of alienation, isolation, and psychological distress.

> Thuy, an Asian American woman, shares her lived experience of the psychological toll of racial discrimination in her workplace. Despite being highly qualified and competent in her role, Thuy often finds herself subjected to microaggressions, stereotyping, and exclusionary behavior from colleagues and supervisors.
>
> Thuy's experience is characterized by feelings of isolation, alienation, and emotional distress resulting from the constant barrage of discriminatory treatment she faces. She describes instances where she is overlooked for promotions and opportunities for career advancement, despite her achievements and contributions to the organization.
>
> Pascoe and Smart Richman's (2009) research has shown that experiences of racial discrimination can have profound psychological effects on individuals, leading to increased levels of stress, anxiety, depression, and other mental health issues. Thuy's experience reflects this reality, as she grapples with feelings of inadequacy, self-doubt, and frustration in response to the discrimination she faces.
>
> The psychological toll of racial discrimination extends beyond the workplace and impacts various aspects of Thuy's life, including her relationships, self-esteem, and overall well-being. She describes how the constant stress and anxiety associated with racial discrimination have taken a toll on her mental health, affecting her ability to concentrate, sleep, and enjoy life outside of work.

Despite the challenges she faces, Thuy remains resilient and determined to advocate for herself and others who experience racial discrimination. She seeks support from friends, family, and mental health professionals to cope with the psychological effects of discrimination and cultivate a sense of empowerment and agency in navigating the challenges she faces.

Thuy's experience underscores the importance of addressing systemic racism and creating inclusive and equitable environments where all individuals feel valued, respected, and supported.

Emotional Impact of Workplace Discrimination

Sue et al. (2017) found workplace discrimination inflicts emotional harm on BIPOC individuals, eroding their sense of belonging, dignity, and self-worth. Experiences of discrimination can evoke a range of emotional responses, including anger, frustration, and helplessness, as individuals grapple with the injustice and indignity of being treated unfairly assert Lewis et al. (2015). Moreover, Cunningham et al. (2014) posit the cumulative effects of discrimination can lead to emotional exhaustion and burnout, as individuals struggle to cope with the stress and strain of navigating a discriminatory work environment. These emotional burdens not only impair job performance and satisfaction but also spill over into other areas of life, affecting relationships, health, and overall quality of life.

Implications for Mental Health and Well-Being

The psychological and emotional toll of workplace discrimination can have profound implications for the mental health and well-being of BIPOC individuals. Paradies et al's (2015) research has consistently found that experiences of discrimination are associated with increased risk of mental health disorders, including depression, anxiety, and substance abuse. Moreover, the chronic stress of coping with discrimination can contribute to physical health problems, such as hypertension, diabetes, and cardiovascular disease, further exacerbating disparities in health outcomes according to Pascoe and Smart Richman (2009). These adverse mental health outcomes not only undermine the productivity and effectiveness of affected individuals but also impose significant costs on society in terms of healthcare utilization and lost productivity.

Lucinda, a Honduran woman, has been working in a corporate environment for several years. Despite her qualifications and dedication to her job, Lucinda experiences persistent microaggressions, discrimination, and exclusionary behavior from her coworkers and supervisors. She notices that she is often overlooked for opportunities for advancement and feels isolated and undervalued in the workplace.

Lucinda's experience exemplifies the detrimental impact of systemic racism on mental health and wellbeing in employment. Research has shown that BIPOC individuals often face higher levels of workplace discrimination, harassment, and stress compared to their white counterparts according to Chang et al. (2018). These experiences of discrimination and marginalization can contribute to increased levels of anxiety, depression, and other mental health issues among BIPOC employees.

In Lucinda's case, the constant microaggressions and exclusionary behavior she faces in the workplace take a toll on her mental health and wellbeing. She struggles with feelings of worthlessness, imposter syndrome, and anxiety about her job security. Despite her efforts to seek support and advocate for herself, Lucinda finds it challenging to navigate the hostile work environment and maintain her overall wellbeing.

Lucinda's experience highlights the intersectional nature of mental health disparities in employment, where race, ethnicity, and gender intersect to create unique challenges and barriers to wellbeing.

As an Asian American woman, Lucinda faces multiple layers of discrimination and marginalization that contribute to her feelings of distress and disempowerment in the workplace.

To address mental health and wellbeing disparities due to systemic racism in the workplace, organizations must take proactive steps to create inclusive and supportive work environments.

This may include implementing diversity and inclusion training, establishing zero-tolerance policies for discrimination and harassment, providing access to mental health resources and support networks, and promoting culturally competent leadership and management practices.

Lucinda's experience underscores the importance of addressing systemic racism in the workplace to promote mental health and wellbeing among BIPOC employees.

In conclusion, systemic racism in employment perpetuates barriers to employment; wage disparities and economic inequality; occupational segregation and limited career advancement; and psychological and emotional harm for BIPOC individuals, contributing to racial inequality within the labor market. Workplace discrimination creates a hostile and stressful work environment that erodes self-esteem, dignity, and resilience, leading to increased risk of mental health disorders and adverse health outcomes. Addressing these effects of systemic racism upon employment requires concerted efforts at the institutional, organizational, and policy levels to promote equity, diversity, and inclusion, and create pathways for economic advancement for all individuals, regardless of race or ethnicity.

Intervention Strategies and Policy Recommendations to Mitigate Systemic Racism in Employment

The following strategies for addressing systemic racism in employment can assist in their dismantlement.

Diversity and Inclusion Initiatives
Diversity and inclusion initiatives play a crucial role in addressing systemic racism in employment by promoting equitable representation and opportunities for underrepresented groups in the workforce state Kalev et al. (2006). These initiatives encompass a range of strategies, including recruitment and hiring practices that prioritize diversity, training programs to foster cultural competency and sensitivity, and mentorship and sponsorship programs to support career advancement for racial minorities assert Pager et al. (2009). By creating inclusive workplace cultures that value and celebrate diversity, organizations can mitigate the effects of systemic racism and promote equal access to opportunities for all employees.

Anti-Discrimination Laws and Enforcement
Strengthening enforcement mechanisms and anti-discrimination laws is essential for combating systemic racism in employment and holding organizations accountable for discriminatory practices according to studies conducted by Pager and Shepherd (2008). Policymakers must enact legislation that prohibits discrimination on the basis of race, ethnicity, gender, and other protected characteristics, and establish robust enforcement mechanisms to investigate complaints and penalize violators suggest Pager et al. (2009). Moreover, Pager and Shepherd concur that policymakers should allocate resources to support agencies responsible for enforcing anti-discrimination

laws and provide training and guidance to employers on compliance with legal requirements. By enhancing legal protections and enforcement efforts, society can deter discriminatory practices and promote equal opportunities for all individuals in the workforce.

Pay Equity and Transparency

Promoting pay equity and transparency is critical for addressing systemic racism in employment and narrowing wage gaps between racial minorities and their white counterparts. Policymakers should enact legislation that mandates pay equity audits and reporting requirements to ensure transparency in compensation practices and identify and address disparities in pay. Moreover, organizations should implement policies that promote equitable pay practices, such as salary banding, standardized pay scales, and performance-based compensation systems, to minimize the influence of bias and discrimination in salary decisions assert Pager et al. (2009). By promoting pay equity and transparency, society can reduce disparities in wages and ensure that all employees receive fair and equitable compensation for their work.

Education and Training Programs

Investing in education and training programs is essential for addressing systemic racism in employment and promoting diversity, equity, and inclusion in the workforce. Employers should provide comprehensive training programs to raise awareness of unconscious bias, cultural competence, and inclusive leadership practices among managers and employees. Moreover, educational institutions should incorporate diversity and inclusion curricula into their programs to prepare students for the diverse and multicultural workforce of the 21st century according to Pager et al. (2009). By fostering awareness and understanding of

systemic racism and its impact on employment, education and training programs can empower individuals
and organizations to create more inclusive and equitable work environments.

Community Engagement and Advocacy
    Community engagement and advocacy are
essential for addressing systemic racism in employment and promoting social justice and equity in the
workforce. Civil rights organizations, advocacy groups,
and grassroots movements play a crucial role in raising
awareness of systemic racism, mobilizing support for
policy reforms, and holding employers and policymakers accountable for promoting diversity and inclusion. Moreover, community-based organizations can
provide support services, resources, and networking
opportunities for racial minorities to empower them to
navigate and overcome systemic barriers to employment according to Pager et al's (2009) research. By
fostering community engagement and advocacy,
society can amplify the voices of marginalized communities and drive meaningful change in the fight against
systemic racism in employment.

    In conclusion, intervention strategies and policy
recommendations are essential for addressing systemic racism in employment and promoting diversity,
equity, and inclusion in the workforce. By implementing
diversity and inclusion initiatives, strengthening anti-
discrimination laws and enforcement mechanisms,
promoting pay equity and transparency, investing in
education and training programs, and fostering
community engagement and advocacy, society can
dismantle systemic barriers to employment and create
more equitable opportunities and outcomes for all
individuals, regardless of race or ethnicity. By working
collaboratively across sectors and with stakeholders,
we can build a more just, inclusive, and equitable

society where every individual has the opportunity to thrive and succeed.

6
Systemic Racism
in Criminal Justice

6
The Impacts of Systemic Racism on the Criminal Justice System

The criminal justice system encompasses the institutions, policies, and practices established by governments to maintain social order, prevent and control crime, and deliver justice. It is primarily composed of three main components: law enforcement, the judiciary, and corrections. Law enforcement includes police and other agencies responsible for investigating crimes, apprehending suspects, and maintaining public safety. They are the first point of contact within the system. The judiciary is comprised of the court system, including prosecutors, defense attorneys, judges, and juries. The judiciary is responsible for ensuring fair trials, interpreting laws, and handing down sentences based on legal statutes and evidence presented. Corrections includes a variety of facilities and programs, such as prisons, jails, probation, and parole systems, which oversee the punishment, rehabilitation, and supervision of convicted offenders. The criminal justice system operates under a framework of laws and regulations designed to protect individual rights and uphold justice. However, the effectiveness and fairness of this system can be influenced by various factors, including legal policies, social norms, and resource availability.

Systemic racism within the criminal justice system refers to the structural and institutional policies, practices, and norms that produce and perpetuate racial inequalities and disparities. Examining the impacts of systemic racism in this context is crucial for several reasons: disproportionate impact; fairness and justice; social and economic consequences; policy reforms; and public health. Addressing systemic racism in criminal justice can thus have broader benefits for community health and well-being. By critically examining and addressing systemic racism within the criminal justice system, society can move towards a more just, equitable, and effective system that better serves all individuals, regardless of race or ethnicity.

Disparities in Policing

Disparities in policing refer to the unequal treatment of individuals based on race, ethnicity, and socioeconomic status, leading to disproportionate targeting and use of force against minority communities. These disparities manifest in practices such as racial profiling, stop-and-frisk, and harsher sentencing for similar offenses committed by people of color compared to their white counterparts. Such systemic biases undermine trust in law enforcement and perpetuate social inequalities within the criminal justice system.

Racial Profiling and Stop-and-Frisk Policies

Racial profiling involves law enforcement targeting individuals for suspicion of crime based on their race, ethnicity, religion, or nationality. Stop-and-frisk policies, notably utilized in New York City, have been criticized for disproportionately targeting minority communities. A study by Gelman, Fagan, and Kiss (2007) found that Black and Latinx individuals were significantly more likely to be stopped and frisked than white individuals.

Alfred Smith, a 22-year-old African American college student, experienced racial profiling firsthand in New York City. On a summer evening, Alfred was walking home from a friend's house in a predominantly white neighborhood. Despite wearing casual clothes and carrying his school backpack, he was stopped by police officers.

The officers approached Alfred with suspicion and immediately demanded to know where he was coming from and where he was headed. Alfred cooperated and politely answered their questions, explaining he was a college student returning home after visiting a friend. Despite his cooperation, the officers insisted on searching his backpack and frisking him.

During the stop-and-frisk, Alfred felt humiliated and fearful. Passersby stared at him, and he felt his dignity being stripped away. The officers found nothing illegal but continued to interrogate him about his presence in the neighborhood. After about fifteen minutes of questioning and searching, they finally let him go without any explanation or apology.

This incident had a profound impact on Alfred. He felt violated and discriminated against solely because of his race. The experience shook his confidence and made him wary of law enforcement. Alfred began to avoid certain neighborhoods and felt anxious whenever he saw police officers.

Stops, Searches, and Arrests

Data consistently show significant racial disparities in police stops, searches, and arrests. According to the Bureau of Justice Statistics (2018), Black drivers were nearly twice as likely to be stopped by police as white drivers. Searches following traffic stops also show disparities, with Black and Latinx drivers more likely to be searched than white drivers, despite lower rates of contraband discovery according to research conducted by Epp, Maynard-Moody, and Haider-Markel (2014).

Sylvia Rodriguez, a 28-year-old Latina, was driving home from work late one evening in a suburban area. Despite following all traffic laws, she was pulled over by a police officer. The officer approached her vehicle with his hand on his holster and asked for her license and registration in a stern manner.

Sylvia complied, providing her documents and asking politely why she was being stopped. The officer did not provide a clear reason and instead asked her to step out of the vehicle for a search. Feeling nervous and confused, Sylvia stepped out and was patted down. The officer then proceeded to search her car without her consent, turning her belongings inside out and causing her significant distress.

During the search, Sylvia was questioned about her destination, her job, and whether she had any illegal substances. Despite finding nothing incriminating, the officer placed her in handcuffs and informed her that she was being arrested for resisting search, even though she had complied with all requests.

The experience left Sylvia feeling violated and deeply mistrustful of law enforcement. She spent several hours in custody before being released without charges, but the emotional trauma remained. Maria found herself becoming anxious whenever she saw police cars and struggled with feelings of anger and helplessness.

Policies Leading to Disproportionate Targeting of Minority Communities

Policies such as "broken windows policing" and aggressive drug enforcement have been criticized for disproportionately targeting minority communities. The War on Drugs, initiated in the 1980s, led to a significant increase in the incarceration of Black and Latinx individuals for drug offenses, despite similar rates of drug use across racial groups purports Alexander (2010). These policies have contributed to mass incarceration and have had long-lasting impacts on minority communities.

Use of Force and Police Violence

The use of force by police disproportionately affects minority communities. Studies have shown that Black individuals are more likely to experience force during police encounters than white individuals. The Bureau of Justice Statistics (2018) reported that Black and Latinx individuals were more likely to be subjected to the threat or use of force by police than white individuals.

Police Shootings and Use of Excessive Force

Research on police shootings indicates significant racial disparities. The Washington Post's database on police shootings shows Black individuals are dispro-portionately represented among those shot and killed by police, relative to their share of the population. Additionally, Fryer (2016) found that Black and Latinx individuals were more likely to experience non-lethal use of force, such as being handcuffed, pushed, or pepper-sprayed, even when not resisting arrest.

John Crawford III, a 22-year-old African American man, experi-enced a tragic encounter with law enforcement in Beavercreek, Ohio. On August 5, 2014, John was shopping in a Walmart store, talking on his cellphone, and carrying an air rifle he had picked up from a store shelf.

A customer called 911, reporting a man was walking around the store with a gun. Although the caller later admitted John was not pointing the rifle at anyone or behaving threateningly, the police responded to the call as an active shooter situation.

Within seconds of arriving at the store, officers Sean Williams and David Darkow encountered John. Despite the lack of immediate threat and without issuing a clear warning or giving John a chance to respond, Officer Williams fired multiple shots, hitting John. John collapsed to the ground, mortally wounded.

John Crawford III was pronounced dead shortly after the shooting. Surveillance footage later showed that John was not behaving aggressively or posing a threat to anyone in the store. The incident had a profound impact on John's family and the community. His death sparked protests and renewed calls for police reform and accountability. The shooting highlighted the dangers of implicit bias and the tendency for law enforcement to use excessive force in situations involving Black individuals.

High-Profile Cases and Their Implications
Several high-profile cases of police violence against Black individuals have brought national attention to the issue of racial disparities in policing. The deaths of Michael Brown in Ferguson, Missouri, Eric Garner in New York City, and George Floyd in Minneapolis have sparked widespread protests and calls for police reform. These cases highlight the urgent need to address systemic racism within law enforcement and have led to policy changes in some jurisdictions, including bans on chokeholds and increased use of body cameras found Khan (2020).

Inequities in Legal Representation
Inequities in legal representation highlight the significant differences in the quality of legal defense provided to individuals based on their financial resources, often resulting in poorer outcomes for those unable to afford private attorneys. Public defenders, burdened with excessive caseloads and limited resources, are often unable to offer the same level of defense as private attorneys, disproportionately affecting low-income and minority defendants. These disparities contribute to higher conviction rates, longer sentences, and an overall lack of justice for disadvantaged groups within the legal system.

Quality Legal Defense
Access to quality legal defense is a critical factor in ensuring fair trials and justice for all individuals. However, systemic inequities often mean that minority defendants face significant barriers in securing competent legal representation. Public defenders, who are appointed to represent those who cannot afford private attorneys, are often overburdened with high caseloads and limited resources. This imbalance compromises their ability to provide effective defense, leading to

poorer outcomes for minority defendants as found in Gideon v. Wainwright according to Gelman, Fagan, and Kiss (2007).

Public Defender Resources versus Private Attorneys

Public defenders typically handle hundreds of cases simultaneously, far exceeding the American Bar Association's recommended caseloads. Farole and Langton (2010) state this overburdening results in limited time and resources for each case, contrasting sharply with private attorneys who generally have more manageable caseloads, better access to investigative and expert resources, and more time to dedicate to each client. Consequently, defendants with private attorneys are more likely to receive thorough representation, which can significantly influence case outcomes.

Luz Hernandez, a 30-year-old Latina, was charged with a non-violent drug offense. Luz had no prior criminal record and maintained she was unaware of the drugs found in her car, which she claimed belonged to a friend. Unable to afford a private attorney, Luz was assigned a public defender.

Luz's public defender was handling over 150 cases simultaneously, leaving limited time to dedicate to each individual client. Due to this overwhelming workload, the public defender had only brief meetings with Luz before her court appearances. These meetings were rushed, and Luz felt she did not have enough time to explain her situation fully or explore all possible defenses.

Despite her innocence, Luz was advised by her public defender to accept a plea deal to avoid the risk of a harsher sentence if convicted at trial. The public defender believed this was the best option given the evidence and the high caseload preventing a thorough investigation.

In contrast, Luz's co-defendant, who could afford a private attorney, had a very different experience. The private attorney conducted an extensive investigation, hired an expert to challenge the prosecution's evidence, and spent significant time preparing a robust defense strategy.

The private attorney also negotiated with the prosecutor more effectively, highlighting mitigating factors and presenting a well-documented case for why the charges should be reduced or dropped. Ultimately, the co-defendant received a much lighter sentence after the private attorney was able to secure a plea deal to a lesser charge.

Luz's experience highlights the disparity between those who rely on public defenders and those who can afford private attorneys. While public defenders are essential and often work tirelessly for their clients, systemic issues like high caseloads and limited resources can hinder their ability to provide the same level of defense as private attorneys.

Case Outcomes for Minority Defendants

The disparity in legal representation quality disproportionately impacts minority defendants. Kutateladze et al's (2014) research indicates that BIPOC defendants are more likely to be represented by public defenders than white defendants. Due to the systemic pressures on public defenders, BIPOC defendants often face higher conviction rates and harsher sentences compared to those who can afford private attorneys. This inequity perpetuates a cycle of disadvantage, as the quality of legal defense directly correlates with the likelihood of acquittal, plea bargaining, and sentencing severity.

Bail and Pretrial Detention

The bail system in the United States further exacerbates disparities in legal outcomes. Defendants unable to afford bail remain in pretrial detention, which undermines their ability to prepare a defense, maintain employment, and care for their families. The inability to secure bail often coerces defendants into accepting plea deals, regardless of their actual guilt, simply to avoid prolonged detention suggests Jones (2013).

Bail Amounts and Pretrial Release

Racial disparities in bail amounts and pretrial release decisions are well-documented. Studies from researchers, such as Reaves (2013), show that minority defendants, particularly Black and Latinx individuals, receive higher bail amounts and are less likely to be granted pretrial release compared to white defendants. These disparities reflect broader systemic biases within the criminal justice system, where minority defendants are often perceived as higher risks, despite similar or lower actual risk levels.

Minority Defendants and Their Families

The consequences of these inequities are profound and multifaceted. Minority defendants who are unable to secure quality legal defense, afford bail, or achieve pretrial release face a higher likelihood of conviction and longer sentences. This disrupts families, as incarceration removes primary caregivers and breadwinners from their homes, leading to financial instability, emotional distress, and adverse outcomes for children report Wildeman and Western (2010). The cumulative effect of these disparities perpetuates social and economic inequalities across generations, undermining community stability and trust in the justice system.

Sentencing Disparities

Sentencing disparities refer to the unequal treatment in sentencing outcomes based on factors such as race, ethnicity, and socioeconomic status. Minority defendants, particularly Black and Latinx individuals, often receive harsher sentences than their white counterparts for similar offenses due to systemic biases within the judicial process. These disparities contribute to the overrepresentation of minorities in the prison system and perpetuate broader social and economic inequalities.

Sentencing for Similar Crimes

Sentencing disparities refer to the unequal treatment of individuals within the criminal justice system, resulting in different sentences for similar crimes based on factors such as race, socioeconomic status, and gender. Research consistently shows that BIPOC inividuals, particularly Black and Latinx, often receive harsher sentences than their white counterparts for comparable offenses. For example, a study by Rehavi and Starr (2014) found that Black men receive sentences that are on average 19.1% longer than those of white men for similar crimes, even after controlling for factors like prior criminal history and the severity of the offense.

Sentencing Lengths and Types

Statistical evidence highlights significant racial disparities in sentencing. According to the United States Sentencing Commission (USSC) (2017), Black male offenders receive sentences that are longer than those of white male offenders for comparable crimes. Additionally, Hispanic offenders also face longer sentences than white offenders, though to a lesser extent. This disparity is evident across various types of crimes, including drug offenses, violent crimes, and property crimes. For example, Black offenders convicted of drug offenses receive sentences that are, on average, nearly 10% longer than those of white offenders (USSC).

James White, a 25-year-old African American man, and David Smith, a 28-year-old white man, were both arrested for possession of a small amount of marijuana in the same jurisdiction. Both men had similar backgrounds with no prior criminal records, and the circumstances of their arrests were nearly identical.

James, following his public defender's advice, pled guilty. The judge sentenced him to six months in jail and a $1,000 fine, citing the need to deter others from similar behavior.

David's private attorney successfully had the charges reduced to a misdemeanor with a recommendation for probation and community service. Ultimately, David received no jail time, a small fine, and 50 hours of community service.

The sentencing disparity between James and David starkly illustrates how racial and socioeconomic factors can influence legal outcomes. Despite similar offenses and backgrounds, the quality of legal representation and implicit biases led to significantly different sentences.

Mandatory Minimum Sentences and Three-Strikes Laws

Mandatory minimum sentences and three-strikes laws contribute significantly to racial disparities in sentencing. Mandatory minimums require judges to impose fixed sentences for specific crimes, often drug-related offenses, regardless of the circumstances. These laws disproportionately impact minority communities. Mauer (2009) notes that mandatory minimums have led to an increase in the incarceration rates of Black and Latinx individuals, who are more likely to be prosecuted for drug offenses. Similarly, three-strikes laws, which impose life sentences on individuals convicted of three or more serious crimes, have been shown to disproportionately affect BIPOC individuals. Research by the Sentencing Project (2018) indicates Black individuals are overrepresented among those sentenced under three-strikes laws.

Prior Convictions and Criminal History

Prior convictions and criminal history play a crucial role in sentencing decisions and exacerbate racial disparities. Offenders with prior convictions are often subject to harsher penalties, and because BIPOC individuals are more likely to have previous criminal records due to systemic biases at earlier stages of the criminal justice process, they are disproportionately affected. Studies conducted by Ulmer (2012) have shown BIPOC with prior convictions receive significantly longer sentences than white offenders with similar records. This cumulative disadvantage results in a cycle of harsher sentencing and higher incarceration rates for minority populations.

Sentencing Decisions Based on Criminal Records
Racial biases, both implicit and explicit, influence sentencing decisions based on criminal records. Judges and juries may unconsciously associate minority defendants with higher levels of dangerousness and culpability, leading to more severe sentences. Research by Bridges and Steen (1998) found that juvenile offenders of color are perceived as more blameworthy and dangerous than their white counterparts, resulting in harsher sentencing recommenddations. Additionally, Eberhardt et al. (2006) demonstrated racial stereotypes about Black defendants, particularly those with more Afrocentric features, lead to harsher sentencing outcomes.

Mass Incarceration
Mass incarceration refers to the extensive and disproportionate imprisonment of individuals, particularly from minority communities, resulting from punitive criminal justice policies. This phenomenon has led to the United States having one of the highest incarceration rates in the world, with significant social and economic impacts on affected communities. The

system of mass incarceration perpetuates cycles of poverty and inequality, as former inmates face numerous barriers to reintegration into society.

Overrepresentation of Minorities in Prison Populations
The overrepresentation of minorities in prison populations is a critical issue in the United States. African Americans and Latinx make up a disproportionate share of the incarcerated population compared to their representation in the general population. This disparity is a result of various factors, including systemic racism, socioeconomic inequalities, and biased law enforcement practices.

Incarceration Rates by Race and Ethnicity
Statistical data reveals significant racial and ethnic disparities in incarceration rates. According to the NAACP (2021), African Americans are incarcerated at more than five times the rate of white individuals. Latinx are also disproportionately affected, with an incarceration rate that is 1.3 times higher than that of whites. The Sentencing Project (2018) highlights that while African Americans and Latinx make up approximately 32% of the U.S. population, they comprise 56% of all incarcerated individuals.

Historical Context and Policy Contributions to Mass Incarceration
The phenomenon of mass incarceration has historical roots and is deeply intertwined with policy decisions made over the past several decades. The War on Drugs, played a significant role in increasing incarceration rates, particularly among BIPOC communities. Alexander (2010) reports policies such as mandatory minimum sentences, three-strikes laws, and zero-tolerance policing disproportionately affect African Americans and Latinx. Additionally, the 1994 Crime Bill contributed to an increase in the prison

population through its provision of funds for the expansion of the prison system and tougher sentencing laws state Mauer and Cole (2018).

Long-term Effects of Incarceration on Minority Communities

The long-term effects of incarceration on minority communities are profound and multifaceted. Formerly incarcerated individuals often face significant barriers to reintegration, including limited employment opportunities, disenfranchisement, and social stigma. These challenges are exacerbated for minorities, who may already be grappling with systemic socioeconomic disadvantages. Incarceration also disrupts family structures, leading to negative outcomes for children and contributing to the perpetuation of cycles of poverty and criminality report Western and Pettit (2010).

Social, Economic, and Familial Impacts

The social, economic, and familial impacts of mass incarceration are extensive. Economically, incarceration reduces earning potential and employment prospects, contributing to higher poverty rates among minority communities. Socially, high incarceration rates erode social capital and community cohesion. Familially, incarceration can lead to the destabilization of family units, with children of incarcerated parents facing a higher risk of behavioral issues, academic struggles, and future involvement with the criminal justice system according to Clear (2007).

Marcus Johnson, an African American man from a low-income neighborhood, was arrested at the age of 22 for possession of a small amount of crack cocaine. This incident was his first offense. Marcus' case occurred during the height of the War on Drugs, a period marked by stringent drug laws and severe penalties for drug-related offenses.

Due to his inability to afford a private attorney, Marcus was represented by a public defender. His public defender, overwhelmed by a heavy caseload, spent minimal time on Marcus's case. Marcus was advised to accept a plea deal, which included a five-year mandatory minimum sentence without the possibility of parole. Given the harsh sentencing guidelines for crack cocaine compared to powder cocaine, Marcus faced significantly longer incarceration than if he had been caught with an equivalent amount of powder cocaine.

Marcus served his full sentence in a high-security prison, surrounded by others convicted of various offenses. During his time in prison, he faced numerous challenges, including limited access to educational and rehabilitative programs. The prison environment was harsh, with frequent violence and a lack of mental health support.

Upon his release, Marcus struggled to reintegrate into society. The stigma of his criminal record made it difficult to find stable employment and housing. He faced social isolation and a lack of support services, which are common issues for formerly incarcerated individuals.

Marcus's story is reflective of the broader impact of mass incarceration on African American communities. The policies that led to his incarceration disproportionately target people of color, contributing to significant racial disparities in the prison population. According to Alexander (2010), mass incarceration has become a modern-day racial caste system, perpetuating economic and social disadvantages for Black Americans.

Parole and Probation: Racial Disparities and Influencing Factors

Parole and probation are forms of community supervision that serve as alternatives to incarceration. While probation typically involves a period of supervision in the community instead of imprisonment, parole is a conditional release from prison before the full sentence is served. Both mechanisms are critical components of the criminal justice system aimed at rehabilitating offenders and reducing prison overcrowding. However, racial disparities in parole decisions and probation terms reflect broader systemic inequalities.

Parole Decisions and Probation Terms

Research consistently shows that racial minorities, particularly Black and Latinx individuals, experience less favorable outcomes in parole and probation decisions compared to their white counterparts. These disparities manifest in various ways:

1. Parole Decisions: Black and Latinx inmates are less likely to be granted parole than white inmates, even when controlling for offense severity, criminal history, and behavior while incarcerated presents Spohn (2015). Studies by Phelps (2000) indicate that parole boards, often comprised predominantly of white members, may harbor implicit biases that influence their decisions, leading to disproportionate denials for minority inmates.

2. Probation Terms: Minority probationers often receive harsher probation conditions, such as more frequent check-ins, mandatory drug testing, and participation in various programs, compared to white probationers. Miller's (2018) research demonstrates these stringent conditions increase the likelihood of technical violations, which can lead to probation revocations and incarceration.

Parole Grant Rates and Probation Conditions by Race
Data illustrates significant racial disparities in parole grant rates and probation conditions:
1. Parole Grant Rates: A study by the U.S. Sentencing Commission (2017) found that Black inmates were 16% less likely to be granted parole compared to white inmates. In some states, the disparity is even more pronounced. For example, in New York, the parole grant rate for Black inmates was approximately 35%, compared to 45% for white inmates according to the New York State Parole Board (2019).
2. Probation Conditions: According to the Bureau of Justice Statistics (2019), Black probationers are subject to more restrictive conditions than their white counterparts. For instance, 60% of Black probationers are required to undergo frequent drug testing, compared to 45% of white probationers. Additionally, Black probationers are more likely to have electronic monitoring and curfews imposed as conditions of their probation.

Disparities in Community Supervision
Several factors contribute to racial disparities in parole and probation:
1. Implicit Bias: Smith and Levinson (2012) posit parole board members and probation officers may hold implicit biases that affect their decisions, consciously or unconsciously favoring white offenders over minorities. These biases can stem from societal stereotypes that associate minority groups with criminality.
2. Structural Inequality: Systemic issues such as socioeconomic disparities, access to legal representation, and differences in community resources play a significant role. Alexander (2010) suggests minority individuals often lack the financial resources to hire private attorneys or enroll in alternative programs that could influence parole or probation outcomes favorably.

3. Policy and Practice: Policies that emphasize punitive measures over rehabilitation disproportionately affect minority communities. For example, zero-tolerance policies and mandatory minimum sentences contribute to higher incarceration and supervision rates for minorities according to Mauer and King (2007).

4. Community Supervision Practices: Probation officers may impose stricter conditions on minority probationers due to perceived risks or stereotypes. Phelps (2020) research documents these practices are often reinforced by a lack of cultural competency and training in recognizing and mitigating biases.

Systemic Racism in Corrections

Systemic racism in corrections manifests in various forms, including the conditions within prisons, treatment of minority inmates, differential treatment, reentry challenges, and recidivism. These issues contribute to the perpetuation of racial inequalities within the criminal justice system and society at large.

Prisons and Treatment of Minority Inmates

Minority inmates often experience harsher conditions and treatment in prisons compared to their white counterparts. These conditions include overcrowding, inadequate healthcare, and limited access to educational and vocational programs. Minority inmates are also more likely to face solitary confinement and other punitive measures disproportionately. According to the Prison Policy Initiative (2018), Black and Latinx inmates are overrepresented in higher-security facilities, which typically have more restrictive environments and fewer rehabilitative opportunities. This disparity in treatment exacerbates the challenges minority inmates face in prison and upon release.

Discrimination, Abuse, and Differential Treatment in Correctional Facilities

Numerous reports have documented the systemic discrimination, abuse, and differential treatment of minority inmates within correctional facilities. These reports highlight instances of physical and verbal abuse, racial profiling, and biased disciplinary actions. For example, a report by the U.S. Department of Justice (2016) found that correctional officers often use excessive force against Black and Latinx inmates at higher rates than white inmates. The report also noted that minority inmates frequently receive harsher punishments for similar infractions, contributing to a climate of mistrust and hostility.

Reentry Challenges and Recidivism

Reentry into society poses significant challenges for minority ex-offenders, who often face systemic barriers to successful reintegration. These barriers include limited access to employment, housing, education, and healthcare, which are critical for successful reentry. Research by the Urban Institute (2015) indicates that minority ex-offenders are less likely to secure stable employment and housing compared to white ex-offenders, due in part to persistent racial discrimination and stigma. This lack of stability increases the risk of recidivism, as ex-offenders struggle to reintegrate into society.

Barriers to Successful Reintegration for Minority Ex-Offenders

Minority ex-offenders face numerous barriers to successful reintegration, including:

Employment: Employers often discriminate against individuals with criminal records, particularly those from minority backgrounds. This discrimination limits job opportunities and economic stability.

Housing: Many housing providers refuse to rent to individuals with criminal records, disproportionately affecting minority ex-offenders. This can lead to homelessness or unstable living conditions.

Education: Access to educational programs and resources is often restricted for ex-offenders, hindering their ability to acquire new skills and improve their prospects.

Healthcare: Minority ex-offenders often lack access to adequate healthcare, including mental health and substance abuse treatment, which are critical for successful reintegration.

Impact of Systemic Racism on Recidivism Rates

Systemic racism significantly impacts recidivism rates among minority ex-offenders. The cumulative effect of discrimination, limited opportunities, and social stigma creates a cycle of disadvantage that increases the likelihood of reoffending. A study by the Sentencing Project (2018) found that Black and Latinx ex-offenders have higher recidivism rates compared to white ex-offenders, largely due to the systemic barriers they face. Addressing these disparities requires comprehensive reforms that tackle the root causes of systemic racism within the criminal justice system.

Policy and Reform in the Criminal Justice System

One significant approach to addressing systemic racism in the criminal justice system involves dismantling policies and practices that perpetuate racial disparities is training law enforcement officers in implicit bias and cultural competency to reduce discriminatory practices states Lawrence (2019). Additionally, data collection and transparency initiatives aim to monitor and address racial disparities in policing, sentencing, and incarceration suggests Alexander (2010).

Legislative and Policy Changes Aimed at Reducing Disparities

Several legislative and policy changes have been enacted to reduce racial disparities in the criminal justice system. The Fair Sentencing Act of 2010, which reduced the sentencing disparity between crack and powder cocaine offenses, is a notable example according to the U.S. Sentencing Commission (2015). More recently, the First Step Act of 2018 aimed to reduce recidivism and reform sentencing laws that disproportionately affected minority communities state Brown (2019). At the state level, policies such as bail reform, decriminalization of minor offenses, and juvenile justice reforms have been implemented to reduce racial disparities and provide alternatives to incarceration found Mauer and King (2007).

Community-Based and Restorative Justice Initiatives

Community-based and restorative justice initiatives offer alternative approaches to traditional punitive measures, focusing on rehabilitation, reconciliation, and community involvement. Zehr's (2002) research demonstrates restorative justice programs facilitate dialogue between offenders and victims, aiming to repair harm and reintegrate offenders into society. Marlowe's (2010) research pinpoints community-based programs, such as diversion initiatives and treatment courts, address underlying issues like substance abuse and mental health, reducing reliance on incarceration and improving outcomes for marginalized populations.

Challenges and Future Directions

Despite progress, significant challenges remain in addressing systemic racism in the criminal justice system. Resistance to change, political polarization, and resource constraints hinder comprehensive reform efforts assert Travis and Western (2014). Additionally, entrenched biases and structural inequalities continue to perpetuate disparities. Future directions for reform include expanding access to legal representation, increasing community engagement in policy-making, and fostering partnerships between law enforcement and marginalized communities attests Weisburd and Neyroud (2011). Sampson (2012) suggests emphasizing prevention and early intervention strategies, such as education and economic development, is also crucial for addressing root causes of criminal behavior and reducing racial disparities.

Ongoing Issues and Areas Needing Further Reform
   Ongoing issues in the criminal justice system that require further reform include racial profiling, mass incarceration, and disparities in sentencing. The school-to-prison pipeline, which disproportionately affects minority youth, remains a critical concern state Wald and Losen (2003). Further reform is needed to address systemic biases in prosecutorial discretion, parole decisions, and reentry support. Enhancing oversight and accountability mechanisms, such as civilian review boards and independent investigations of police misconduct, is essential for building trust and ensuring justice contends Walker (2001).

Call to Action for Addressing Systemic Racism in the Criminal Justice System
   Addressing systemic racism in the criminal justice system requires a multifaceted approach, encompassing legislative changes, community-based initiatives, and ongoing efforts to dismantle structural inequalities. While progress has been made, continued advocacy, research, and policy innovation are necessary to achieve a more equitable and just system. Here are key calls to action to advance this agenda:

1. Legislative and Policy Reforms
Implementing Fair Sentencing Practices: Reform sentencing laws to eliminate disparities, such as the disproportionate penalties for crack versus powder cocaine offenses. Alexander (2010) suggests this includes revisiting mandatory minimum sentences and three-strikes laws that disproportionately impact minority communities.

Bail Reform: Replace cash bail with risk assessment tools to reduce pretrial detention rates, which disproportionately affect low-income and minority defendants. Jurisdictions should adopt policies that prioritize non-monetary release options contends Stevenson (2018).

Decriminalization of Minor Offenses: Decriminalize or reclassify low-level, non-violent offenses such as drug possession to reduce incarceration rates and provide more proportionate responses to these offenses suggests Mauer and King (2007).

2. Law Enforcement Reforms
Bias Training and Cultural Competency: Mandate comprehensive training for law enforcement officers on implicit bias, cultural competency, and de-escalation techniques. This training should be ongoing and continuously evaluated for effectiveness according to Lawrence (2019).

Increased Accountability: Establish independent oversight bodies to investigate police misconduct and use of force incidents. Walker (2001) suggests strengthening civilian review boards and implement body-worn camera policies to enhance transparency.

Community Policing Initiatives: Foster partnerships between police departments and community organizations to build trust and improve public safety. Weisburd and Neyroud (2011) assert community policing should focus on collaborative problem-solving and proactive engagement.

3. Judicial and Prosecutorial Reforms

Diversifying the Judiciary: Increase the diversity of judges and prosecutors to ensure that the criminal justice system reflects the communities it serves. Spohn (2013) posits diverse representation can lead to more equitable decision-making.

Eliminating Racial Bias in Prosecutions: Implement policies to monitor and address racial disparities in charging decisions, plea bargains, and sentencing recommendations. Prosecutors should be trained to recognize and mitigate implicit biases according to Davis (2017).

Sentencing Reform: Advocate for sentencing guidelines that promote rehabilitation over punishment and consider the social and economic contexts of offenders. Zehr (2002) states this includes expanding alternatives to incarceration, such as community service, treatment programs, and restorative justice initiatives.

4. Community and Restorative Justice Initiatives

Restorative Justice Programs: Expand the use of restorative justice practices that involve victims, offenders, and community members in resolving conflicts and addressing the harm caused by criminal behavior. These programs focus on healing and reintegration rather than punishment state Zehr (2002).

Community-Based Diversion Programs: Support community-based diversion programs that provide alternatives to formal criminal justice processing for low-level offenders, particularly youth. According to Marlowe (2010), these programs should include access to education, employment, and mental health services.

Reentry Support Services: Enhance support for individuals reentering society after incarceration. This includes providing access to housing, employment, education, and mental health care to reduce recidivism and support successful reintegration posit Travis and Western (2014).

5. Data Collection and Research
Comprehensive Data Collection: Mandate the collection and public reporting of comprehensive data on arrests, charges, sentencing, and incarceration rates disaggregated by race and ethnicity. This data is crucial for identifying and addressing disparities contends Balko (2018).

Ongoing Research: Support ongoing research to examine the effectiveness of reforms and identify best practices for reducing racial disparities in the criminal justice system. This research should inform policy and practice suggests Sampson (2012).

7
Systemic Racism
in Housing

7
Impacts of Systemic Racism on Housing

Homeownership has long been a cornerstone of wealth accumulation in the United States, yet systemic racism has significantly hindered the ability of BIPOC individuals to attain and benefit from homeownership at the same rates as their white counterparts. Systemic racism in housing refers to the entrenched policies, practices, and societal norms that perpetuate racial inequities in access to housing, homeownership, and neighborhood quality. This chapter examines the historical and contemporary impacts of systemic racism on housing disparities. The roots of housing disparities are deeply embedded in historical practices such as redlining and racially restrictive covenants. Redlining, initiated in the 1930s by the Home Owners' Loan Corporation, involved marking neighborhoods predominantly inhabited by African Americans and other minorities as high-risk for mortgage lending as stated in research by Massey and Denton (1993). Redlining, a practice where banks and insurers denied loans and insurance to residents in predominantly BIPOC neighborhoods, severely restricted their ability to purchase homes and invest in their communities. These practices effectively denied generations of BIPOC families the opportunity to purchase homes and build wealth, leading to concentrated poverty and segregation assert Rothstein (2017).

Access to Housing
Access to housing is significantly impeded by discriminatory practices that perpetuate racial dispa-rities in homeownership. These practices, including redlining and biased lending, disproportionately affect marginalized communities, exacerbating socioecono-

mic inequalities and limiting their access to safe and affordable housing.

Discriminatory Lending Practices

Modern discriminatory lending practices continue to restrict access to housing for BIPOC individuals. Studies by Munnell, Tootell, Browne, and McEneaney (1996) have shown that BIPOC applicants are more likely to be denied mortgages or offered loans with less favorable terms compared to their white counterparts, even when they have similar financial profiles. These practices limit the ability of BIPOC individuals to purchase homes and build wealth, contributing to significant disparities in homeownership rates.

Housing Affordability and Wealth Disparities

Systemic racism also contributes to disparities in housing affordability. Desmond's research demonstrates (2016) BIPOC communities are more likely to experience higher housing costs relative to their income, leading to housing instability and a greater risk of eviction. Wealth disparities exacerbate this issue, as BIPOC households typically have lower levels of wealth and savings compared to white households, making it more difficult to afford down payments and secure housing in desirable areas claim Shapiro, Meschede, and Osoro (2013).

Limited Access to Affordable Housing

Access to affordable housing is another significant barrier for BIPOC communities. Discriminatory practices in the allocation of affordable housing resources, such as Section 8 vouchers and public housing, often result in these communities being concentrated in high-poverty, low-opportunity neighborhoods Schwartz (2010) contends. These areas typically have limited access to quality schools, healthcare, and employment opportunities, further entrenching social and economic inequalities.

Housing Quality and Conditions

Housing quality is significantly impacted by discriminatory practices, leading to stark disparities in living conditions between racial groups. Historically rooted practices have resulted in minority communities often residing in substandard housing with limited access to essential resources and services.

Disparities in Housing Quality

BIPOC individuals are more likely to live in substandard housing conditions compared to their white counterparts. Homes in predominantly BIPOC neighborhoods frequently lack essential amenities and are in poorer condition due to systemic disinvestment found Massey and Denton (1993). Issues such as inadequate heating, plumbing problems, and structural deficiencies are more prevalent in these communities, exacerbating health risks and reducing quality of life according to Krieger and Higgins' (2002) research.

Environmental Hazards

Systemic racism also exposes BIPOC communities to greater environmental hazards. Many marginalized neighborhoods are located near industrial sites, landfills, and other sources of pollution, leading to higher levels of environmental toxins in these areas according to Bullard et al. (2007). Residents are consequently at increased risk for respiratory illnesses, lead poisoning, and other health problems associated with poor environmental quality state Brulle and Pellow (2006).

Access to Amenities and Services
The quality of housing in BIPOC neighborhoods is further compromised by limited access to essential services and amenities. These areas often lack adequate public transportation, healthcare facilities, grocery stores, and recreational spaces, contributing to a lower overall quality of life attests Wilson (1987). This disparity in access not only affects day-to-day living conditions but also limits economic opportunities and social mobility.

Homeownership and Wealth Accumulation
Home ownership has long been considered a cornerstone of wealth accumulation in America, yet discriminatory practices and biased lending policies have systematically denied this opportunity to many racial minorities. These inequities have perpetuated significant racial wealth gaps, hindering economic mobility and stability for affected communities.

Mortgage Discrimination and Lending Practices
Even after the passage of the Fair Housing Act of 1968, which aimed to eliminate housing discrimination, Quillian et al. found (2020) BIPOC individuals continue to face significant barriers in accessing mortgage loans. Studies have shown that lenders are more likely to deny mortgage applications from Black and Latino applicants, even when they have similar credit profiles and financial qualifications as white applicants. Additionally, BIPOC homeowners often receive less favorable loan terms, including higher interest rates and fees, which further exacerbates the wealth gap contend Munnell et al. (1996).

Wealth Disparities and Home Equity
Homeownership is a key mechanism for building and transferring wealth across generations. However,

systemic racism has limited the ability of BIPOC families to accumulate home equity at the same rate as white families. Perry et al's (2018) research indicates that homes in predominantly Black neighborhoods appreciate in value more slowly than those in predominantly white neighborhoods, reducing the potential for wealth accumulation through property appreciation. Consequently, BIPOC homeowners often have less home equity and are more vulnerable to economic downturns and housing market fluctuations.

Intergenerational Wealth Transfer
The racial wealth gap is perpetuated through disparities in homeownership and home equity, which influence the ability of families to transfer wealth across generations. According to Shapiro (2024), white families are more likely to benefit from inter-generational transfers of wealth, including financial assistance for down payments and inheritances, which facilitate homeownership and wealth accumulation. In contrast, BIPOC families, who have been historically excluded from these opportunities, face greater challenges in achieving economic stability and mobility.

Neighborhood Effects

Discriminatory practices in housing and lending have long-lasting neighborhood effects, perpetuating cycles of poverty and segregation. These practices result in unequal access to resources and opportunities, further entrenching systemic inequities within marginalized communities.

Discriminatory Housing Policies
Redlining was complemented by other discriminatory policies, including racial covenants in property deeds that prohibited the sale of homes to non-white buyers, and urban renewal projects that displaced

minority communities found Massey and Denton (1993). The Fair Housing Act of 1968 aimed to eliminate these practices, but enforcement has been inconsistent, allowing de facto segregation to persist.

Economic and Social Impacts

The segregation of neighborhoods by race has created stark disparities in wealth accumulation, educational opportunities, and access to essential services. Minority neighborhoods often suffer from lower property values, underfunded schools, and inadequate public services. This systemic disinvestment perpetuates cycles of poverty and limits upward mobility for residents assert Sharkey (2013).

Health and Environmental Effects

Residents of segregated neighborhoods also face greater health risks due to exposure to environmental hazards, limited access to healthcare facilities, and higher crime rates. Williams and Collins (2001) suggest the concentration of poverty and lack of resources contribute to higher rates of chronic illnesses and mental health issues among minority populations.

Current Challenges and Policy Responses

Despite legal advancements, racial segregation in neighborhoods remains a pervasive issue. Efforts to address this include enforcing fair housing laws, promoting affordable housing development in diverse areas, and supporting community-led initiatives to improve neighborhood conditions state Pfeiffer (2020). Policymakers and advocates emphasize the need for comprehensive strategies that address both historical injustices and contemporary inequalities.

Legal and Policy

Discriminatory practices in housing are deeply embedded in legal and policy frameworks that have historically favored certain racial groups over others. These systemic inequities perpetuate disparities and hinder efforts towards achieving true equality and justice in society.

Fair Housing Act of 1968

The Fair Housing Act (FHA) of 1968 was a landmark piece of legislation aimed at eliminating housing discrimination and promoting residential integration. The Act prohibits discrimination in the sale, rental, and financing of housing based on race, color, national origin, religion, sex, familial status, and disability. Despite its significance, enforcement of the FHA has been inconsistent, and discriminatory practices continue in more covert forms found Yinger (1995).

Discriminatory Lending Practices

Contemporary discriminatory lending practices, such as subprime lending and mortgage discrimination, have perpetuated housing inequities. The Dodd-Frank Wall Street Reform of 2010 and the Consumer Protection Act of 2010 introduced measures to address these issues, including the establishment of the Consumer Financial Protection Bureau to oversee and enforce fair lending laws.

Current Policy Challenges

Despite legal protections, systemic racism in housing persists through various mechanisms, including zoning laws, discriminatory real estate practices, and inequitable access to housing resources. Zoning laws, for example, often segregate communities by race and income by restricting affordable housing development in affluent areas found Rothwell and Massey (2009).

> Marcia Johnson, a middle-aged African American woman living in Chicago, experienced discriminatory lending practices that significantly impacted her ability to afford housing. Marcia had a stable job, a good credit score, and was ready to buy her first home. However, her journey was fraught with challenges that exemplify the systemic racism embedded in the housing finance sector.
>
> Marcia initially approached several banks to apply for a mortgage. Despite her strong financial background, she noticed that the terms offered to her were consistently less favorable compared to her white colleagues with similar or even weaker financial profiles. She was offered higher interest rates, additional fees, and less favorable loan conditions. These terms made it difficult for her to secure an affordable mortgage, increasing the long-term cost of homeownership.
>
> During her search, Marcia found a suitable home in a predominantly African American neighborhood. However, she soon realized that lenders were reluctant to finance homes in her desired area, a practice known as redlining. This form of discrimination involves denying services or charging more for services based on the racial or ethnic composition of the neighborhood.
>
> Marcia's loan officer subtly hinted that she might get better terms if she chose a home in a "different" (implicitly, whiter) neighborhood. This suggestion reinforced the discriminatory barriers she faced, as it limited her housing options and further perpetuated segregation.
>
> Due to the discriminatory lending practices, Marcia faced significantly higher monthly mortgage payments and higher overall costs, which strained her financial resources. The higher interest rates and additional fees increased the total cost of her loan by tens of thousands of dollars over its term. This financial burden limited her ability to invest in other areas, such as saving for retirement or her children's education.

The experience took a psychological toll on Marcia. The repeated discrimination she faced left her feeling disheartened and marginalized. She reported feeling like a second-class citizen, not worthy of the same financial opportunities as her white peers. This sense of disenfranchisement contributed to stress and anxiety, impacting her overall wellbeing.

Marcia's experience is not unique. Studies have shown that African Americans are often subjected to discriminatory lending practices, which contribute to the racial wealth gap and ongoing residential segregation. For example, research by the Center for Responsible Lending (CRL) found that African Americans were more likely to be offered subprime loans even when they qualified for prime loans. This systemic issue highlights the need for stronger regulatory oversight and enforcement of fair lending laws. Marcia Johnson's experience underscores the pervasive nature of discriminatory lending practices and their profound impact on housing affordability and financial stability for minority communities.

Policy Recommendations to Mitigate the Impacts of Systemic Racism in Housing

Addressing these deeply rooted issues within housing requires comprehensive policy reforms and robust enforcement mechanisms. The following policy recommendations aim to mitigate the impacts of systemic racism in housing.

Strengthening Enforcement of Fair Housing Laws

- Enhanced Oversight by HUD and CFPB: The Department of Housing and Urban Development (HUD) and the Consumer Financial Protection Bureau (CFPB) should receive increased funding and resources to rigorously enforce fair housing and lending laws. Strengthening these agencies' capacities will ensure that discriminatory practices are identi-

fied and addressed promptly (Dodd-Frank Act, 2010).
- Data Collection and Transparency: Implement mandatory reporting requirements for lenders, real estate agencies, and landlords to provide detailed data on housing transactions. Turner et al. (2013) suggest transparency in housing data will help identify patterns of discrimination and facilitate targeted interventions.

Promoting Inclusive Zoning Policies
- Inclusionary Zoning: Municipalities should adopt inclusionary zoning policies that require a percentage of new housing developments to be affordable for low- and moderate-income families. Inclusionary zoning can promote socioeconomic diversity and reduce segregation state Schuetz, Meltzer, and Been (2009).
- Reforming Exclusionary Zoning Laws: Repeal or amend exclusionary zoning laws that restrict the development of affordable housing in affluent neighborhoods. These reforms will allow for a more equitable distribution of housing opportunities across urban and suburban areas suggest Rothwell and Massey (2009).

Increasing Affordable Housing Funding
- Federal and State Funding: Increase federal and state funding for the construction and maintenance of affordable housing. Programs such as the Low-Income Housing Tax Credit should be expanded to incentivize private developers to build affordable units contends Eriksen (2009).
- Housing Vouchers: Expand the Section 8 Housing Choice Voucher Program to assist more low-income families in accessing quality housing. Improving voucher portability will

enable families to move to neighborhoods with better opportunities insist Collinson, Ellen, and Ludwig (2016).

Supporting Community Land Trusts

- Community Land Trusts (CLTs): Promote the establishment of CLTs to provide permanent, affordable housing and prevent displacement. Davis (2010) found CLTs maintain community ownership of land, which can stabilize neighborhoods and ensure long-term affordability.
- Public-Private Partnerships: Encourage partnerships between local governments, nonprofits, and private investors to support CLTs and other community-driven housing initiatives. Gray and Galande (2011) believe collaborative efforts can leverage resources and expertise to enhance housing affordability and stability.

Addressing Environmental Inequities

- Environmental Justice Policies: Develop policies that address the environmental hazards disproportionately affecting minority communities. Ensuring that new affordable housing developments are located in safe, healthy environments is critical for equitable housing according to Bullard et al. (2007).
- Remediation Programs: Invest in programs to remediate environmental hazards in existing housing, particularly in communities of color. Efforts to improve housing conditions can significantly enhance residents' health and well-being attest Evans and Kantrowitz (2002).

Enhancing Homeownership Opportunities

- Down Payment Assistance: Provide down payment assistance and other financial support for first-time homebuyers from minority communities. Such programs can help overcome the initial barriers to homeownership and promote wealth building assert Herbert et al. (2005).

- Credit Access Programs: Develop programs to improve access to credit for minority home-buyers. Offering financial education and assistance with credit repair can help more families qualify for mortgages state Apgar and Calder (2005).

8
Thriving Amidst Systemic Racism

8
Thriving Amidst Systemic Racism: Strategies for Success among BIPOC Individuals

As previously demonstrated in Chapters Three-Seven, systemic racism remains a pervasive and deeply entrenched issue in various sectors of society, presenting significant challenges for Black, Indigenous, and People of Color (BIPOC) individuals. However, despite facing systemic barriers, many BIPOC individuals have demonstrated **resilience, resourcefulness, and determination** in navigating these obstacles to achieve success in their personal and professional lives.

This comprehensive chapter explores a myriad of strategies and approaches that BIPOC individuals can employ to not only survive but thrive amidst systemic racism. Drawing on empirical research, theoretical frameworks, and practical insights, this chapter provides a comprehensive roadmap for BIPOC individuals to overcome systemic barriers, leverage their strengths, and achieve their goals. By examining factors such as personal responsibility, education, career advancement, mental health, community support, and advocacy, this chapter offers a holistic perspective on how BIPOC individuals can navigate the complexities of systemic racism and **emerge stronger, more empowered, and more successful**.

Prior to examining the specific strategies, there are two crucial factors impacting individual success: autonomy and agency. Both play crucial roles in addressing and dismantling systemic racism from an inner mental perspective. Autonomy refers to the ability of individuals or groups to make their own decisions and act independently, embodying the essence of independent thinking and the courage to deviate from the status quo. It involves exercising the freedom to choose one's path and make decisions that reflect personal values and beliefs, unencumbered by external pressures or societal expectations. Agency, on the other hand, signifies the capacity of individuals to exert power, make informed choices, and take decisive actions that shape their own lives and influence the world around them. It encompasses the personal strength and determination to challenge existing power structures and advocate for fundamental rights and justice. By asserting their agency, individuals stand against oppression and inequity, driving social change and transforming their circumstances and communities. Together, autonomy and agency empower people to navigate and reshape their environments, fostering resilience, self-determination, and collective empowerment in the pursuit of equity and justice.

In the context of systemic racism, autonomy and agency are often undermined or usurped within marginalized communities. Systemic racism refers to the ways in which societal systems and structures perpetuate racial inequality, often resulting in disparities in areas such as education, employment, housing, and criminal justice. These systems can limit and/or squelch the autonomy of individuals by creating barriers to opportunities and resources based on race. Empowering individuals and communities to exercise their autonomy and agency is essential in combating systemic racism. Overall, autonomy and agency are essential for individuals and communities to challenge systemic racism, dismantle oppressive structures, and create a more just and equitable society. By empowering people to recognize their own power and take action, we can work towards a future where everyone has the unencumbered freedom to live with dignity, regardless of their race or ethnicity.

In addition to employing autonomy and agency, it is crucial for individuals to possess self-awareness and a positive self-esteem from which personal responsibility can be activated. Promoting healthy self-esteem in individuals is vital for enabling them to thrive amidst the challenges posed by systemic racism. Systemic racism can severely impact one's sense of self-worth and identity, making it essential to cultivate a strong, positive self-image. Here are three strategies to foster healthy self-esteem in individuals facing systemic racism:

1. Education and Awareness: Providing comprehensive education about the history and impact of systemic racism can help individuals understand that their experiences of discrimination are not personal failures but the result of broader societal issues. Knowledge empowers individuals to contextualize their experiences and resist internalizing negative stereotypes.

2. Skill Development: Offering opportunities for skill development and education can enhance individuals' confidence in their abilities and future prospects. Programs that provide training, scholarships, and career development can open new pathways and increase self-esteem.

3. Recognition and Validation: Acknowledging and validating an individual's experiences and achievements can reinforce their sense of worth. Celebrating successes, both big and small, helps build a positive self-image and counters the negative impacts of systemic racism. Furthermore, instillment of intrinsic value and motivation has far reaching effects, such as being self-motivated and self-driven in attaining one's goals.

Despite the challenges posed by discrimination, many racial minorities employ adaptive coping strategies and resilience mechanisms to navigate and cope with adversity attest Chavous et al. (2003) in congruence with autonomy, agency, and a healthy self-esteem. Seeking social support, cultivating a strong sense of ethnic identity, and engaging in activism and advocacy are all strategies that individuals use to resist and challenge discrimination, reclaiming a sense of agency and empowerment in the face of adversity purport Mendoza-Denton et al. (2002). Moreover, Chen and Miller (2012) assert interventions aimed at promoting psychological resilience and well-being, such as mindfulness-based stress reduction programs and culturally sensitive therapy, can help individuals cope with the psychological and emotional effects of discrimination and build resilience in the face of adversity. Additionally, strategies in the following arenas have proved useful for many.

Education as a Foundation for Success

Education serves as a critical foundation for success, providing BIPOC individuals with the knowledge, skills, and opportunities necessary to thrive in a competitive world. However, Harper and Gasman (2008) found systemic racism in education manifests in various forms, including unequal access to quality education, racial bias in academic settings, and limited representation of BIPOC perspectives in curricula. To overcome these challenges, Griffin and Gilbert (2010) contend that BIPOC individuals can advocate for equitable access to education, seek out mentorship and support networks, and leverage resources such as scholarships and financial aid to pursue higher education. Additionally, fostering a strong sense of cultural identity and pride can empower BIPOC students to navigate academic spaces with confidence and resilience according to Oyserman et al. (2003).

Career Advancement and Professional Development

Pager et al's (2009) research indicates that in the workplace, BIPOC individuals often face systemic barriers to career advancement, including racial bias in hiring and promotion practices, unequal access to opportunities for skill development and advancement, and workplace discrimination. To overcome these challenges, Hunt et al., (2018) contend BIPOC individuals can actively seek out opportunities for professional development, such as mentorship programs, leadership training, and networking events. Additionally, advocating for diversity and inclusion initiatives within organizations can help create more equitable workplaces that value and support the contributions of BIPOC employees assert Cox and Blake (1991). By investing in their professional growth and advocating for systemic change, BIPOC individuals can position themselves for success in their careers.

Mental Health and Well-Being
The experience of systemic racism can take a toll on the mental health and well-being of BIPOC individuals, leading to increased levels of stress, anxiety, and depression according to Paradies et al. (2015). To prioritize their mental health, BIPOC individuals can engage in self-care practices such as mindfulness, meditation, and exercise, which can help reduce stress and promote emotional well-being state Chen and Miller (2012). From their research, Sue et al. (2007) found seeking support from mental health professionals, community organizations, and support networks can also provide BIPOC individuals with the resources and guidance they need to address their mental health needs. Additionally, Kim et al. (2003) believe advocating for culturally competent mental health services and policies can help ensure that BIPOC individuals have access to quality care that respects their cultural backgrounds and experiences.

Community Support and Advocacy
Community support and advocacy play a crucial role in empowering BIPOC individuals to navigate systemic racism and achieve success. Building strong

support networks within BIPOC communities can provide individuals with emotional support, mentorship, and resources to help them overcome systemic barriers contend Chavous et al. (2008). Additionally, engaging in collective action and advocacy efforts can help BIPOC individuals address systemic injustices and advocate for policy changes that promote equity and justice according to Lewis et al. (2015). By mobilizing their communities and amplifying their voices, BIPOC individuals can effect meaningful change and create a more inclusive and equitable society for future generations.

Political Participation

Political participation is the cornerstone of democratic societies, offering individuals the opportunity to wield their agency in shaping policies and institutions. Encouraging robust political engagement empowers citizens to not only voice their concerns but also actively participate in the decision-making processes that shape their communities and the broader society. This involvement spans various forms, including the fundamental act of voting, the courageous step of running for public office to represent one's values and vision, and the tireless advocacy for policies that tackle systemic racism head-on and champion equity for all. By fostering a culture of political participation, we empower individuals to become catalysts for change, driving forward progress towards a more just and inclusive society where every voice is heard and every person's rights are upheld.

Economic Empowerment

Supporting economic empowerment initiatives represents an investment in the resilience and potential of marginalized communities. By fostering entrepreneurship, offering comprehensive job training programs, and facilitating access to capital, we not only provide the necessary resources but also cultivate an environment where individuals can flourish. Economic empowerment serves as a catalyst for autonomy, liberating individuals from the shackles of discriminatory systems and opening doors to self-sufficiency and prosperity. Moreover, it lays the groundwork for financial stability and long-term wealth accumulation, affording individuals the freedom to pursue their aspirations and secure their futures. Through these initiatives, we not only address immediate economic disparities but also sow the seeds for sustainable growth and equitable opportunities, ensuring that all members of society have the chance to thrive and contribute to collective prosperity.

Cultural Expression and Representation
Cultural expression and representation serve as powerful vehicles for marginalized communities to reclaim their narratives and assert their rightful place in society's tapestry. By nurturing cultural expression and ensuring diverse representation, we not only challenge harmful stereotypes but also catalyze transformative social change. Embracing cultural autonomy empowers individuals to celebrate their rich heritage and craft inclusive spaces where their voices resonate with authenticity and respect. Through these acts of self-affirmation, marginalized communities transcend mere visibility to cultivate meaningful connections, fostering empathy, understanding, and solidarity across societal divides. By amplifying diverse voices and narratives, we foster a culture of belonging and mutual respect, paving the way for a more equitable and harmonious society where every individual's story is cherished and every cultural heritage is celebrated as a source of strength and inspiration.

All of the aforementioned strategies will empower minority individuals, granting them a higher rate of success in their personal and professional endeavors, procuring a seat at the decision-making table, and ensuring that their collective voices are heard and valued. By fostering healthy self-esteem through education, cultural affirmation, mentorship, strong support networks, mental health resources, empowerment programs, positive representation, advocacy, skill development, and recognition, we create a foundation for marginalized communities to actively participate in shaping policies and societal structures. This inclusive approach not only amplifies diverse perspectives but also drives meaningful change towards equity and justice, ultimately transforming the landscape to reflect the true diversity and strength of our society.

References

Agency for Healthcare Research and Quality. (2018).
National healthcare disparities report.

Alexander, M. (2010). *The New Jim Crow: Mass
Incarceration in the Age of Colorblindness.* The
New Press.

Altonji, J. G., & Blank, R. M. (1999). Race and gender
in the labor market. *Handbook of Labor Economics*
3, 3143-3259.

American Civil Liberties Union of Michigan. (2018).
Kids under the gun: An ACLU of Michigan report
on the quality of education in Detroit.

Andersen, M. L., & Hill Collins, P. (2015). Race,
Class, and Gender: An Anthology. Wadsworth
Publishing.

Anderson, J. D. (2015). The education of blacks in the
South, 1860-1935. UNC Press Books.

Apgar, W., & Calder, A. (2005). The dual mortgage
market: The persistence of discrimination in
mortgage lending. In X. de Souza Briggs (Ed.),
*The geography of opportunity: Race and
housing choice in metropolitan America.* 101-123.
Brookings Institution Press.

Artiga, S., Orgera, K., & Damico, A. (2016). Changes
in health coverage by race and ethnicity since
implementation of the ACA, 2013-2015.

Austin, S. (2023). U.S. Supreme Court Ends
Affirmative Action in Higher Education: An
Overview and Practical Next Steps for Employers.
sidley.com.

Baicker, K., Chandra, A., & Skinner, J. S. (2017).
Geographic variation in health care and the
problem of measuring racial disparities.
Perspectives on Biology and Medicine, 60(2), 199-
226.

Baker, B. D., & Corcoran, S. P. (2012). The Stealth
Inequities of School Funding: How State and Local

Finance Systems Perpetuate Inequitable Student Spending. Center for American Progress.

Baker, B. D., & Welner, K. G. (2011). School Finance and Courts: Does Reform Matter, and How Can We Tell? *Teachers College Record*, 113(11), 2382-2423.

Bakker, A. B., & Demerouti, E. (2007). The job demands-resources model: State of the art. *Journal of Managerial Psychology*, 22(3), 309-328.

Bailey, Z. D., Krieger, N., Agénor, M., Graves, J., Linos, N., & Bassett, M. T. (2017). Structural racism and health inequities in the USA: Evidence and interventions. *The Lancet*, 389(10077), 1453-1463.

Balko, R. (2018). *Rise of the warrior cop: The militarization of America's police forces.* Public Affairs.

Banks, J. A. (1993). Multicultural education: Historical development, dimensions, and practice. *Review of Research in Education*, 19(1), 3-49.

Bartik, T. J., & Lachowska, M. (2012). The Short-Term Effects of School Quality on Labor Market Outcomes: Evidence from the 1999 North Carolina School Accountability Program. Upjohn Institute Working Paper No. 12-181.

Battiste, M. (2013). Decolonizing education: Nourishing the learning spirit. Saskatoon, SK: Purich Publishing.

Baum, S., & Steele, P. (2010). The Effects of College on the Earnings of African American and White Students. In *The Black-White Achievement Gap*, 225-255. Brookings Institution Press.

Bell, D. (1980). Brown v. Board of Education and the interest-convergence dilemma. *Harvard Law Review*, 93(3), 518-533.

Bertrand, M., and Mullainathan, S. (2004). Are Emily and Greg More Employable Than Lakisha and Jamal? A Field Experiment on Labor Market Discrimination. *The American Economic Review*,

94(4), 991-1013.

Betancourt, J. R., Green, A. R., Carrillo, J. E., & Ananeh-Firempong II, O. (2003). Defining cultural competence: A practical framework for addressing racial/ethnic disparities in health and health care. *Public Health Reports*, 118(4), 293-302.

Blau, F. D., & Kahn, L. M. (2017). The gender wage gap: Extent, trends, and explanations. *Journal of Economic Literature*, 55(3), 789-865.

Bonilla-Silva, E. (2017). Racism without Racists: Color-Blind Racism and the Persistence of Racial Inequality in the United States. Rowman & Littlefield.

Bor, J., Venkataramani, A. S., Williams, D. R., & Tsai, A. C. (2018). Police killings and their spillover effects on the mental health of black Americans: A population-based, quasi-experimental study. *The Lancet*, 392(10144), 302-310.

Bowen, W. G., & Bok, D. (1998). *The Shape of the River: Long-Term Consequences of Considering Race in College and University Admissions*. Princeton University Press.

Bowen, W. G., Chingos, M. M., & McPherson, M. S. (2009). Crossing the finish line: Completing college at America's public universities. *Princeton University Press.*

Brach, C., & Fraser, I. (2000). Can cultural competency reduce racial and ethnic health disparities? A review and conceptual model. *Medical Care Research and Review*, 57(Suppl 1), 181-217.

Braveman, P., Egerter, S., & Williams, D. R. (2011). The social determinants of health: Coming of age. *Annual Review of Public Health*, 32, 381-398.

Brayboy, B. M., & Castagno, A. E. (2008). Self-determination through self-education: Culturally responsive schooling for Indigenous students in the USA. *Teaching Education*, 19(1), 75-96.

Bridges, G. S., & Steen, S. (1998). Racial disparities in

official assessments of juvenile offenders: Attributional stereotypes as mediating mechanisms. *American Sociological Review, 63*(4), 554-570. https://doi.org/10.2307/2657267

Brown, E. (2019). The First Step Act of 2018: Risk and needs assessment system. *Federal Probation, 83*(1), 26-35.

Brulle, R. J., & Pellow, D. N. (2006). Environmental justice: Human health and environmental inequalities. *Annual Review of Public Health, 27*, 103-124.

Bullard, R. D., Johnson, G. S., & Torres, A. O. (2007). *Environmental health and racial equity in the United States: Building environmentally just, sustainable, and livable communities.* American Public Health Association.

Bullard, R. D., Mohai, P., Saha, R., & Wright, B. (2007). Toxic wastes and race at twenty: Why race still matters after all of these years. *Environmental Law, 38*, 371-411.

Bureau of Justice Statistics. (2018). Contacts between police and the public, 2015. Retrieved from https://www.bjs.gov/content/pub/pdf/cpp15.pdf

Bureau of Justice Statistics. (2019). *Probation and Parole in the United States.* Retrieved from https://www.bjs.gov/index.cfm?ty=pbdetail&iid=6986

Burgess, D. J., Ding, Y., Hargreaves, M., van Ryn, M., Phelan, S., & Dovidio, J. (2008). The association between perceived discrimination and underutilization of needed medical and mental health care in a multi-ethnic community sample. *Journal of Health Care for the Poor and Underserved, 19*(3), 894-911.

Camangian, P. R. (2012). Toward a critical pedagogy of race. *Race Ethnicity and Education, 15*(1), 71-87.

Carnevale, A. P., et al. (2015). *Recovery: Job Growth*

and Education Requirements through 2020. Georgetown University Center on Education and the Workforce.

Chang, E. C., Chang, O. D., Martos, T., Sallay, V., Lee, J., & Stam, K. R. (2018). Discrimination, harassment, and well-being: A systematic review. *Journal of Counseling Psychology, 65*(4), 437–454.

Chavous, T. M., Rivas-Drake, D., Smalls, C., Griffin, T., & Cogburn, C. (2008). Gender matters, too: The influences of school racial discrimination and racial identity on academic engagement outcomes among African American adolescents. *Developmental Psychology, 44*(3), 637.

Chen, J. A., & Miller, G. E. (2012). Socioeconomic status and health: mediating and moderating factors. *Annual Review of Clinical Psychology, 9,* 723-749.

Chetty, R., Friedman, J. N., Saez, E., Turner, N., & Yagan, D. (2017). Mobility report cards: The role of colleges in intergenerational mobility (No. w23618). National Bureau of Economic Research.

Clear, T. R. (2007). *Imprisoning Communities: How Mass Incarceration Makes Disadvantaged Neighborhoods Worse.* Oxford University Press.

Cohen, J. J., Gabriel, B. A., & Terrell, C. (2002). The case for diversity in the health care workforce. *Health Affairs, 21*(5), 90-102.

Collinson, R., Ellen, I. G., & Ludwig, J. (2016). Low-income housing policy. *Economics of Means-Tested Transfer Programs in the United States, Volume I.* https://doi.org/10.3386/w21071

Cox, T., & Blake, S. (1991). Managing cultural diversity: Implications for organizational competitiveness. *Academy of Management Executive, 5*(3), 45-56.

Crenshaw, K. (1989). Demarginalizing the intersection of race and sex: A Black feminist critique of antidiscrimination doctrine, feminist theory and antiracist politics. *University of Chicago Legal Forum*, 139-167.

Cuevas, A. G., O'Brien, K., & Saha, S. (2016). What is health equity? And what difference does a definition make? *Journal of Health Disparities Research and Practice*, *9*(2), 154-167.

Cunningham, T. J., Berkman, L. F., & Kawachi, I. (2014). Occupational differences in self-rated health: a comparison of the relationship in working and non-working populations. Journal of *Epidemiology & Community Health*, *68*(6), 550-556.

Darity Jr, W., Castellino, D. R., & Hamilton, D. (2006). For those who've come across the seas: Race, ethnicity, and the adaptation of immigrant descendants. *International Migration Review*, 40(3), 748-794.

Davis, A. J. (2017). *Policing the Black man: Arrest, prosecution, and imprisonment*. Pantheon.

Davis, A. Y. (2019). *Women, Race, & Class*. Vintage Books.

Davis, J. E. (2010). *The community land trust reader*. Lincoln Institute of Land Policy.

Delgado, R., & Stefancic, J. (2017). *Critical race theory: An introduction*. NYU Press.

Desmond, M. (2016). *Evicted: Poverty and profit in the American city*. Crown.

DiAngelo, R. (2018). *White Fragility: Why It's So Hard for White People to Talk About Racism*. Beacon Press.

Dodd-Frank Wall Street Reform and Consumer Protection Act, Pub. L. No. 111-203, 124 Stat. 1376 (2010).

Downey, D. B., & Pribesh, S. (2004). When race matters: Teachers' evaluations of students' classroom behavior. *Sociology of Education*, 277-301.

Duncan, G. J., & Murnane, R. J. (2014). Restoring opportunity: The crisis of inequality and the challenge for American education. *Harvard University Press.*

Duncan, G. J., & Murnane, R. J. (2011). *Whither Opportunity?: Rising Inequality, Schools, and Children's Life Chances.* Russell Sage Foundation.

Eberhardt, J. L., Davies, P. G., Purdie-Vaughns, V. J., & Johnson, S. L. (2006). Looking deathworthy: Perceived stereotypicality of Black defendants predicts capital-sentencing outcomes. *Psychological Science, 17*(5), 383-386. https://doi.org/10.1111/j.1467-9280.2006.01716.x

Epp, C. R., Maynard-Moody, S., & Haider-Markel, D. P. (2014). *Pulled over: How police stops define race and citizenship.* University of Chicago Press.

Eriksen, M. D. (2009). The market price of low-income housing tax credits. *Journal of Urban Economics, 66*(2), 141-149.

Evans, G. W., & Kantrowitz, E. (2002). Socioeconomic status and health: The potential role of environmental risk exposure. *Annual Review of Public Health, 23*(1), 303-331.

Fair Housing Act, 42 U.S.C. §§ 3601-3619 (1968).

Farole, D. J., & Langton, L. (2010). County-based and Local Public Defender Offices, 2007. Bureau of Justice Statistics.

Ferguson, R. F. (2001). Teachers' perceptions and expectations and the Black-White test score gap. *Urban Education, 36*(4), 466-507.

Fernandez, R. M., & Castilla, E. J. (2020). Networks, Diversity, and Economic Mobility. *Annual Review of Sociology*, 46, 581-604.

FitzGerald, C., & Hurst, S. (2017). Implicit bias in healthcare professionals: A systematic review. *BMC Medical Ethics, 18*(1), 19.

Fryer, R. G. (2016). An empirical analysis of racial

differences in police use of force. *Journal of Political Economy, 127*(3), 1210-1261. doi:10.1086/701423

Gamble, V. N., Aarons, S., Guyot, J., & Qureshi, A. (2018). Moving the needle: Multisectoral collaboration as a way to advance racial equity in health care. *American Journal of Public Health, 108*(S5), S385-S387.

Gay, G. (2010). Culturally Responsive Teaching: Theory, Research, and Practice. *Teachers College Press*.

Gelman, A., Fagan, J., & Kiss, A. (2007). An analysis of the New York City Police Department's "stop-and-frisk" policy in the context of claims of racial bias. *Journal of the American Statistical Association, 102*(479), 813-823. doi:10.1198/016214506000001040 Gideon v. Wainwright, 372 U.S. 335 (1963).

Giroux, H. A. (1992). Border crossings: Cultural workers and the politics of education. Routledge.

Goldrick-Rab, S. (2016). Paying the price: College costs, financial aid, and the betrayal of the American dream. University of Chicago Press.

Gottlieb, L. M., Tirozzi, K. J., & Manchanda, R. (2016). The Nuka System of Care: Improving health through ownership and relationships. *International Journal of Circumpolar Health, 75*(1), 33893.

Gray, K. A., & Galande, M. (2011). Keeping "community" in a community land trust. *Social Work Research, 35*(4), 241-248.

Green, A. R., Carney, D. R., Pallin, D. J., Ngo, L. H., Raymond, K. L., Iezzoni, L. I., & Banaji, M. R. (2007). Implicit bias among physicians and its prediction of thrombolysis decisions for Black and White patients. *Journal of General Internal Medicine, 22*(9), 1231-1238.

Gregory, A., Clawson, K., Davis, A., & Gerewitz, J. (2016). The promise of restorative practices to transform teacher-student relationships and achieve equity in school discipline. *Journal of Educational and Psychological Consultation, 26*(3), 325-353.

Griffin, K. A., & Gilbert, C. G. (2010). Fostering the success of all students: Moving beyond race as a proxy for disadvantage. *The Educational Forum, 74*(1), 28-39.

Grogan, M., & Shakeshaft, C. (2011). *Women and educational leadership.* John Wiley & Sons.

Hall, S. et al. (2013). *Representation: Cultural Representations and Signifying Practices.* Sage Publications.

Harper, S. R., & Gasman, M. (2008). Consequences of conservatism: Black male students and the politics of historically Black colleges and universities. *The Journal of Negro Education, 77*(4), 336-351.

Harper, S. R., & Gasman, M. (2008). *Historically Black Colleges and Universities: What You Should Know.* Stylus Publishing, LLC.

Harper, S. R., & Hurtado, S. (2007). Nine themes in campus racial climates and implications for institutional transformation. *New Directions for Student Services, 2007*(120), 7-24.

Heckman, J. J., et al. (2010). *The Rate of Return to the High/Scope Perry Preschool Program.* NBER Working Paper.

Herbert, C. E., Haurin, D. R., Rosenthal, S. S., & Duda, M. (2005). Homeownership gaps among low-income and minority borrowers and neighborhoods. *Cityscape, 8*(1), 17-53.

Hoffman, K. M., Trawalter, S., Axt, J. R., & Oliver, M. N. (2016). Racial bias in pain assessment and treatment recommendations, and false beliefs about biological differences between Blacks and Whites. *Proceedings of the National Academy of Sciences, 113*(16), 4296-4301.

Howard, T. C. (2010). *Why race and culture matter in*

schools: Closing the achievement gap in America's classrooms. Teachers College Press.

Howard, T. C. (2018). *Culturally responsive teaching: Theory, research, and practice*. Teachers College Press.

Howell, E. A., Egorova, N., Balbierz, A., Zeitlin, J., & Hebert, P. L. (2016). Black-white differences in severe maternal morbidity and site of care. *American Journal of Obstetrics and Gynecology*, 214(1), 122.e1-122.e7.

Hunt, V., Layton, D., & Prince, S. (2018). *Diversity Matters*. McKinsey & Company. Retrieved from https://www.mckinsey.com/business-functions/organization/our-insights/delivering-through-diversity.

Hurtado, S., Alvarez, C. L., Guillermo-Wann, C., Cuellar, M., & Arellano, L. (2012). A model for diverse learning environments. *New Directions for Student Services*, 2012(138), 5-16.

Ingersoll, R. M., & May, H. (2011). Recruitment, Retention and the Minority Teacher Shortage. Consortium for Policy Research in Education.

Irizarry, J. G. (2016). *The Latinization of U.S. schools: Successful teaching and learning in shifting cultural contexts*. Harvard University Press.

Israel, B. A., Schulz, A. J., Parker, E. A., & Becker, A. B. (2003). Review of community-based research: Assessing partnership approaches to improve public health. *Annual Review of Public Health*, 19(1), 173-202.

Jackson, C. K., & Bruegmann, E. (2009). Teaching students and teaching each other: The importance of peer learning for teachers. *American Economic Journal: Applied Economics*, 1(4), 85-108.

Jones, C. E. (2013). "Give Us Free": Addressing Racial Disparities in Bail Determinations. *New York University Journal of Legislation and Public Policy*, 16(4), 919-963.

Jones, C. P., & Wells, K. B. (2007). Strategies for academic and clinician engagement in community-participatory partnered research. *JAMA, 297*(4), 407-410.

Jones, J. et al. (2010). *Labor of Love, Labor of Sorrow: Black Women, Work, and the Family, from Slavery to the Present.* Basic Books.

Jones, J. H., Bayer, R., & Fairchild, A. L. (2008). The Tuskegee legacy: AIDS and the black community. *American Journal of Public Health, 98*(6), 994-1000.

Kalev, A., Dobbin, F., & Kelly, E. (2006). Best practices or best guesses? Assessing the efficacy of corporate affirmative action and diversity policies. *American Sociological Review, 71*(4), 589-617.

Kendi, I. X. (2016). *Stamped from the Beginning: The Definitive History of Racist Ideas in America.* Bold Type Books.

Khan, A. (2020). Chokeholds, duty to intervene: The major police reforms prompted by George Floyd's death. *NPR.* Retrieved from https://www.npr.org/sections/live-updates-protests-for-racial justice/2020/06/16/877253974/chokeholds-duty-to-intervene-the-major-police-reforms-prompted-by-george-floyds-death

Kim, J., Chan, M. M., & Park, S. Y. (2003). Cultural competence in action: Addressing and mitigating healthcare disparities. *Pediatric Nursing, 29*(5), 389-392.

Kober, N., & Rentner, D. S. (2011). State funding of schools and equity: A national overview of current formulas. Center on Education Policy.

Kochhar, R., Fry, R., & Rohal, M. (2016). Wealth inequality has widened along racial, ethnic lines since end of Great Recession. Pew Research Center.

Krieger, J., & Higgins, D. L. (2002). Housing and

health: Time again for public health action. *American Journal of Public Health, 92*(5), 758-768.

Kutateladze, B. L., Andiloro, N. R., Johnson, B. D., & Spohn, C. (2014). Cumulative Disadvantage: Examining Racial and Ethnic Disparity in Prosecution and Sentencing. *Criminology, 52*(3), 514-551.

Ladson-Billings, G. (1995). But that's just good teaching! The case for culturally relevant pedagogy. *Theory into Practice, 34*(3), 159-165.

Ladson-Billings, G. (1995). Toward a theory of culturally relevant pedagogy. *American Educational Research Journal*, 32(3), 465-491.

Ladson-Billings, G. (1998). Just what is critical race theory and what's it doing in a nice field like education? *International Journal of Qualitative Studies in Education, 11*(1), 7-24.

Ladson-Billings, G. (2006). From the Achievement Gap to the Education Debt: Understanding Achievement in U.S. Schools. *Educational Researcher, 35*(7), 3-12.

Ladson-Billings, G. (2014). Culturally relevant pedagogy 2.0: Aka the remix. *Harvard Educational Review, 84*(1), 74-84.

Lawrence, R. G. (2019). Implicit bias in policing. *Annual Review of Criminology, 2*, 233-254.

Lewis, J. A., Mendenhall, R., Harwood, S. A., & Huntt, M. B. (2015). Coping with gendered racial microaggressions among black women college students. *Journal of African American Studies, 19*(1), 38-52.

Lewis, T. T., Cogburn, C. D., & Williams, D. R. (2015). Self-reported experiences of discrimination and health: scientific advances, ongoing controversies, and emerging issues. *Annual Review of Clinical Psychology*, 11, 407-440.

Losen, D. J., & Martinez, T. E. (2013). Out of school

and off track: The overuse of suspensions in American middle and high schools. The Civil Rights Project at UCLA.

Marlowe, D. B. (2010). Drug court practitioner fact sheet: Research update on adult drug courts. *National Association of Drug Court Professionals.*

Massey, D. S., & Denton, N. A. (1993). *American apartheid: Segregation and the making of the underclass.* Harvard University Press.

Mauer, M. (2009). The changing racial dynamics of the war on drugs. *The Sentencing Project.* Retrieved from https://www.sentencingproject.org/wp-content/uploads/2016/01/Changing-Racial-Dynamics-of-the-War-on-Drugs.pdf

Mauer, M., & Cole, D. (2018). *The Meaning of Life: The Case for Abolishing Life Sentences.* The New Press.

Mauer, M., & King, R. S. (2007). A 25-year quagmire: The War on Drugs and its impact on American society. *The Sentencing Project.*

Mauer, M., & King, R. S. (2007). *Uneven justice: State rates of incarceration by race and ethnicity.* The Sentencing Project.

Mendoza-Denton, R., Downey, G., Purdie, V. J., Davis, A., & Pietrzak, J. (2002). Sensitivity to status-based rejection: Implications for African American students' college experience. *Journal of Personality and Social Psychology, 83*(4), 896.

Miller, R. J. (2018). *Halfway home: Race, punishment, and the afterlife of mass incarceration.* University of California Press.

Minkler, M., & Wallerstein, N. (2008). Community-based participatory research for health: From process to outcomes. John Wiley & Sons.

Morris, E. W. & Perry, B. L. (2016). The Punishment Gap: School Suspension and Racial Disparities in Achievement. *Social Problems, 63*(1), 68–86.

Morrison, B., Vaandering, D., & Zanoni, L. (2010).

Restorative justice in the classroom: Fostering responsibility, healing, and hope in the classroom. *Education Canada, 50*(3), 18-21.

Munnell, A. H., Tootell, G. M. B., Browne, L. E., & McEneaney, J. (1996). Mortgage lending in Boston: Interpreting HMDA data. *The American Economic Review, 86*(1), 25-53.

NAACP. (2021). *Criminal Justice Fact Sheet.* Retrieved from https://naacp.org/resources/criminal-justice-fact-sheet

National Fair Housing Alliance. (2018). *Fair Housing Act 50th Anniversary: The state of fair housing.* Retrieved from https://nationalfairhousing.org/

New York State Parole Board. (2019). *Annual Report.* Retrieved from https://www.parole.ny.gov/annualreport.html

Nieto, S. (2000). Affirming diversity: The sociopolitical context of multicultural education. Longman.

Noguera, P. A. (2008). *The Trouble with Black Boys: And Other Reflections on Race, Equity, and the Future of Public Education.* John Wiley & Sons.

Oakes, J., and Lipton, K.. (2003). *Teaching to Change the World.* McGraw-Hill Education.

Orfield, G., & Eaton, S. E. (1996). *Dismantling Desegregation: The Quiet Reversal of Brown v. Board of Education.* New Press.

Orfield, G., & Lee, C. (2005). Historic Reversals, Accelerating Resegregation, and the Need for New Integration Strategies. UCLA Civil Rights Project.

Orfield, G., & Lee, C. (2005). Why Segregation Matters: Poverty and Educational Inequality. The Civil Rights Project at Harvard University.

Oyserman, D., Gant, L., & Ager, J. (1995). A socially contextualized model of African American identity: Possible selves and school persistence. *Journal of Personality and Social Psychology, 69*(6), 1216.

Pager, D, & Shepherd, H.. 2008. The Sociology of Discrimination: Racial Discrimination in Employment, Housing, Credit, and Consumer Markets. *Annual Review of Sociology, 34*, 181-209.

Pager, D., Western, B., & Bonikowski, B. (2009). Discrimination in a Low-Wage Labor Market: A Field Experiment. *American Sociological Review, 74*(5), 777-799.

Paradies, Y., Ben, J., Denson, N., Elias, A., Priest, N., Pieterse, A., ... & Gee, G. (2015). Racism as a determinant of health: A systematic review and meta-analysis. *PloS one, 10*(9), e0138511.

Parker, L., Patton, D. U., & Parker, L. (2013). African Americans and education: A reference handbook. ABC-CLIO.

Pascoe, E. A., & Smart Richman, L. (2009). Perceived discrimination and health: a meta-analytic review. *Psychological Bulletin, 135*(4), 531.

Perez Huber, L., & Solorzano, D. (2015). Racial microaggressions as a tool for critical race research. *Race Ethnicity and Education, 18*(3), 297-320.

Perry, A. M., Rothwell, J., & Harshbarger, D. (2018). *The devaluation of assets in Black neighborhoods: The case of residential property.* Brookings Institution. https://www.brookings.edu/research/devaluation-of-assets-in-black-neighborhoods/

Pfeiffer, D. (2020). Redefining affordable housing: Integrating income- and race-conscious policies. *Housing Policy Debate, 30*(5), 770-792.

Phelps, M. S. (2020). *Mass probation: Toward a more robust theory of state variation in punishment.* Punishment & Society, 22(1), 27-47. https://doi.org/10.1177/1462474519844338

Prison Policy Initiative. (2018). *Mass incarceration: The*

whole pie 2018. Retrieved from https://www.prisonpolicy.org/reports/pie2018.html

Quillian, L., Lee, J. J., & Honoré, B. (2020). Racial Discrimination in the U.S. Housing and Mortgage Lending Markets: A Quantitative Review of Trends, 1976-2016. *Race and Social Problems, 12*(1), 13-28.

Reardon, S. F. (2011). The Widening Academic Achievement Gap Between the Rich and the Poor: New Evidence and Possible Explanations. In R. Murnane & G. Duncan (Eds.), *Whither Opportunity? Rising Inequality, Schools, and Children's Life Chances* (pp. 91-116). Russell Sage Foundation.

Reardon, S. F., & Owens, A. (2014). 60 years after Brown: Trends and consequences of school segregation. *Annual Review of Sociology*, 40, 199-218.

Reardon, S. F., & Portilla, X. A. (2016). Recent trends in income, racial, and ethnic school readiness gaps at kindergarten entry. *AERA Open*, 2(3), 2332858416657343.

Reaves, B. A. (2013). Felony Defendants in Large Urban Counties, 2009 - Statistical Tables. Bureau of Justice Statistics.

Rehavi, M. M., & Starr, S. B. (2014). Racial disparity in federal criminal sentences. *Journal of Political Economy, 122*(6), 1320-1354. https://doi.org/10.1086/677255

Reskin, B. F., & McBrier, D. B. (2000). Why not ascription? Organizations' employment of male and female managers. *American Sociological Review, 65*(2), 210-233.

Reskin, B. F., & Roos, P. A. (1990). Job queues, gender queues: Explaining women's inroads into male occupations. Temple University Press.

Rothstein, R. (2017). *The Color of Law: A Forgotten History of How Our Government Segregated*

America. Liveright Publishing Corporation.

Rothwell, J. T., & Massey, D. S. (2009). The effect of density zoning on racial segregation in U.S. urban areas. *Urban Affairs Review, 44*(6), 779-806.

Saha, S., Taggart, S. H., Komaromy, M., & Bindman, A. B. (2000). Do patients choose physicians of their own race? *Health Affairs, 19*(4), 76-83.

Sampson, R. J. (2012). Great American city: Chicago and the enduring neighborhood effect. University of Chicago Press.

Schuetz, J., Meltzer, R., & Been, V. (2009). 31 Flavors of Inclusionary Zoning: Comparing policies from San Francisco, Washington, DC, and suburban Boston. *Journal of the American Planning Association, 75*(4), 441-456.

Schwartz, A. F. (2010). *Housing policy in the United States*. Routledge.

Sentencing Project. (2018). *Report to the United Nations on racial disparities in the U.S. criminal justice system*. Retrieved from https://www.sentencingproject.org/publications/un-report-on-racial-disparities/

Shapiro, T. M. (2004). *The Hidden Cost of Being African American: How Wealth Perpetuates Inequality*. Oxford University Press.

Shapiro, T. M., Meschede, T., & Osoro, S. (2013). The roots of the widening racial wealth gap: Explaining the black-white economic divide. *Institute on Assets and Social Policy*.

Sharkey, P. (2013). *Stuck in place: Urban neighborhoods and the end of progress toward racial equality*. University of Chicago Press.

Siddle-Walker, V. (1996). Bringing theory to life: Students' perceptions of the teaching of Southern history. *Theory and Research in Social Education, 24*(1), 56-72.

Skiba, R. J., Arredondo, M. I., & Williams, N. T. (2011). More than a metaphor: The contribution of exclusionary discipline to a "school-to-prison pipeline". *Equity & Excellence in Education, 44*(4), 546-564.

Skiba, R. J., Michael, R. S., Nardo, A. C., & Peterson, R. L. (2002). The color of discipline: Sources of racial and gender disproportionality in school punishment. *The Urban Review, 34*(4), 317-342.

Sleeter, C. E. (1993). How white teachers construct race. In C. E. Sleeter & P. L. McLaren (Eds.), Multicultural education, critical pedagogy, and the politics of difference, 156-184. SUNY Press.

Smedley, B. D., Butler, A. S., & Bristow, L. R. (2003). In the nation's compelling interest: Ensuring diversity in the health-care workforce. National Academies Press.

Smith, L. T. (1999). Decolonizing methodologies: Research and indigenous peoples. Zed Books.

Smith, R. J., & Levinson, J. D. (2012). The impact of implicit racial bias on the exercise of prosecutorial discretion. *Seattle University Law Review, 35*, 795-826.

Smith, S. et al. 2017. "Structural Racism and Health Inequities in the USA: Evidence and Interventions." *The Lancet, 389*(10077), 1453-1463.

Snowden, L. R. (2001). Barriers to effective mental health services for African Americans. *Mental Health Services Research, 3*(4), 181-187.

Spohn, C. (2013). Racial disparities in prosecution, sentencing, and punishment. *Crime and Justice, 43*(1), 207-255.

Spohn, C. (2015). *Race, ethnicity, and sentencing*. Oxford University Press.

Stansfeld, S., & Candy, B. (2006). Psychosocial work environment and mental health—a meta-analytic review. *Scandinavian Journal of Work, Environment & Health, 32*(6), 443-462.

Stern, A. M. (2005). Sterilized in the name of public

health: Race, immigration, and reproductive control in modern California. *American Journal of Public Health, 95*(7), 1128-1138.

Stevenson, B. (2018). *Just Mercy: A story of justice and redemption.* Spiegel & Grau.

Sue, D. W., Capodilupo, C. M., Torino, G. C., Bucceri, J. M., Holder, A. M., Nadal, K. L., & Esquilin, M. (2007). Racial Microaggressions in Everyday Life: Implications for Clinical Practice. *American Psychologist, 62*(4), 271-286.

Sue, S., Cheng, J. K. Y., Saad, C. S., & Chu, J. P. (2009). Asian American mental health: A call to action. *American Psychologist, 64*(6), 496-510.

Sue, S., Cheng, J. K. Y., Saad, C. S., & Chu, J. P. (2012). Asian American mental health: A call to action. *American Psychologist,* 67(7), 532-544.

Swail, W. S., Redd, K. E., & Perna, L. W. (2005). Retaining minority students in higher education: A framework for success. *ASHE Higher Education Report, 31*(3), 1-122.

Szasz, M. C., & Carpenter, C. (2012). Indigenous education through dance and ceremony: A Navajo case study. *American Indian Culture and Research Journal, 36*(2), 103-130.

Tomaskovic-Devey, D., Zimmer, C., Stainback, K., Robinson, C., Taylor, T., & McTague, T. (2006). Documenting desegregation: Segregation in American workplaces by race, ethnicity, and sex, 1966-2003. *American Sociological Review, 71*(4), 565-588.

Travis, J., & Western, B. (2014). The growth of incarceration in the United States: Exploring causes and consequences. *National Research Council.*

Truth and Reconciliation Commission of Canada. (2015). Honouring the truth, reconciling for the future: Summary of the final report of the Truth and Reconciliation Commission of Canada.

Turner, M. A., Santos, R., Levy, D. K., Wissoker, D., Aranda, C. L., Pitingolo, R., & The Urban Institute. (2013). *Housing discrimination against racial and ethnic minorities 2012*. U.S. Department of Housing and Urban Development.

Ulmer, J. T. (2012). Revisiting the racial threat hypothesis: The role of police organizational characteristics in the production of racial disparities in the use of deadly force. *Journal of Crime and Justice, 35*(1), 68-99. https://doi.org/10.1080/0735648X.2012.672547

Urban Institute. (2015). *Understanding the challenges of prisoner reentry: Research findings from the Urban Institute's Prisoner Reentry Portfolio.* Retrieved from https://www.urban.org/sites/default/files/publicatio n/42051/413591-Understanding-the-Challenges-of-Prisoner-Reentry.PDF

U.S. Department of Justice. (2016). *Investigation of the Baltimore City Detention Center.* Retrieved from https://www.justice.gov/crt/file/877936/download

U.S. Government Accountability Office. (2018). K-12 EDUCATION: Better Use of Information Could Help Agencies Identify Disparities and Address Racial Discrimination. GAO-18-258.

U.S. Sentencing Commission. (2015). Report to the Congress: Impact of the Fair Sentencing Act of 2010.

U.S. Sentencing Commission. (2017). *Demographic differences in sentencing: An update to the 2012 Booker Report.* Retrieved from https://www.ussc.gov/research/research-reports/demographic-differences-sentencing

Wald, J., & Losen, D. J. (2003). Defining and redirecting a school-to-prison pipeline. *New Directions for Youth Development, 2003*(99), 9-15.

Walker, S. (2001). *Police accountability: The role of civilian oversight.* Wadsworth Publishing.

Wallace, M. E., Mendola, P., & Chen, Z. (2016). The role of socioeconomic status and community social capital on maternal health outcomes in Asian and Pacific Islander Americans. *Maternal and Child Health Journal, 20*(10), 2030-2039.

Warren, M. R., & Mapp, K. L. (2011). *A match on dry grass: Community organizing as a catalyst for school reform.* Oxford University Press.

Washington, H. A. (2006). *Medical apartheid: The dark history of medical experimentation on Black Americans from colonial times to the present.* Anchor Books.

The Washington Post. (n.d.). Fatal Force database. Retrieved from https://www.washingtonpost.com/graphics/investigations/police-shootings-database/

Watson, A. C., Hanrahan, C. F., & Luchins, D. J. (2018). COVID-19, policing, and reform: Realigning our approach to mental health. *Psychiatric Services, 71*(7), 723-726.

Weisburd, D. & Neyroud, P. (2011). *Police science: Toward a new paradigm.* Harvard Kennedy School Program in Criminal Justice Policy and Management.

Western, B., & Pettit, B. (2010). Incarceration & social inequality. *Daedalus, 139*(3), 8-19.

Whaley, A. L. (2001). Cultural mistrust: An important psychological construct for diagnosis and treatment of African Americans. *Professional Psychology: Research and Practice, 32*(6), 555-562.

Wildeman, C., & Western, B. (2010). Incarceration in Fragile Families. *The Future of Children, 20*(2), 157-177.

Williams, D. R., & Collins, C. (2001). Racial residential segregation: A fundamental cause of racial disparities in health. *Public Health Reports, 116*(5), 404-416.

Williams, D. R., González, H. M., Neighbors, H., Nesse, R., Abelson, J. M., Sweetman, J., & Jackson, J. S. (2007). Prevalence and distribution of major depressive disorder in African Americans, Caribbean Blacks, and Non-Hispanic Whites: Results from the National Survey of American Life. *Archives of General Psychiatry, 64*(3), 305-315.

Williams, D. R., & Mohammed, S. A. (2009). Discrimination and racial disparities in health: Evidence and needed research. *Journal of Behavioral Medicine,* 32(1), 20-47.

Williams, D. R., & Mohammed, S. A. 2013. "Racism and Health I: Pathways and Scientific Evidence." *American Behavioral Scientist, 57*(8), 1152-1173.

Williams, D. R., & Wyatt, R. (2015). Racial bias in health care and health: Challenges and opportunities. *Journal of the American Medical Association, 314*(6), 555-556.

Wilson, W. J. (1987). The truly disadvantaged: The inner city, the underclass, and public policy. University of Chicago Press.

Wilson, W. J. (2009). More than Just Race: Being Black and Poor in the Inner City. W.W. Norton & Company.

World Health Organization. (2010). Healthy workplaces: A model for action: For employers, workers, policymakers and practitioners. World Health Organization.

Yinger, J. (1995). *Closed doors, opportunities lost: The continuing costs of housing discrimination.* Russell Sage Foundation.

Zehr, H. (2002). *The little book of restorative justice.* Good Books.

About the Author

Dr. Cassundra White-Elliott is a dynamic and multi-faceted individual, excelling in various roles as an educator, English professor, author, publisher, and minister. With a strong foundation in education, literature, and faith-based leadership, Dr. White-Elliott has dedicated her career to fostering growth, empowerment, spiritual awareness, and social change.

Starting her academic journey with a Bachelor of Arts in Education, Dr. White-Elliott laid the groundwork for her passion for teaching and learning. She recognized the power of education as a tool for transformation and dedicated herself to empowering students to reach their full potential.

Building upon her undergraduate studies, Dr. White-Elliott pursued a Master of Arts in English Composition, delving deep into the intricacies of writer's agency and voice. Armed with a keen understanding of the written word, she honed her skills as a writer, educator, and advocate for marginalized voices in literature.

Continuing her quest for knowledge and expertise, Dr. White-Elliott earned her Ph.D. in Education, specializing in curriculum development and professional studies. Her doctoral research focused on African American English Vernacular and educational biases against its use.

As an educator, Dr. White-Elliott brings passion, creativity, and expertise to her role as an English professor. Through engaging lectures, thought-provoking discussions, and innovative teaching methods, she inspires students to explore the complexities of literature, language, and culture while fostering critical thinking and empathy.

Outside of academia, Dr. White-Elliott is a prolific author, using her writing to amplify marginalized voices and advocate for social change. Her published works span a wide range of genres, from scholarly articles and essays to faith-based and fictional novels, exploring themes of spirituality and social justice.

Driven by a desire to provide a platform for underrepresented writers, Dr. White-Elliott founded a publishing company (CLF Publishing Collaborative, LLC), dedicated to promoting diverse voices and empowering authors to share their stories with the world. As the founder and CEO, she strives to challenge stereotypes, dismantle barriers, and foster understanding and empathy across diverse communities.

In addition to her academic and literary pursuits, Dr. White-Elliott is also a dedicated minister, guiding individuals on their spiritual journeys and fostering a sense of community and belonging. With a focus on love, compassion, and individual growth, she uses her platform as a minister to advocate for the Body of Christ to operate in the spirit of unity while fulfilling their God-given callings.

Overall, Dr. Cassundra White-Elliott's journey is a testament to the power of education, writing, and faith in driving positive change in the world. Through her dedication, passion, and unwavering commitment to changing lives, she continues to inspire others to embrace learning, celebrate diversity, and work towards a more just and equitable society.

Index

afford 27, 53, 54, 55, 58, 65, 68
affordability 29, 65, 69, 70
affordable 18, 27, 39, 65, 67, 68, 69, 70, 83
African 17, 18, 26, 41, 42, 44, 51, 53, 56, 57, 58, 65, 68,
    69, 76, 78, 81, 82, 83, 84, 86
agencies 14, 19, 39, 48, 51, 69, 85
agency 18, 33, 34, 46, 72, 73, 74, 76
aimed 9, 10, 12, 14, 18, 21, 23, 29, 58, 60, 61, 66, 67,
    68, 73
Alexander 5, 52, 57, 58, 59, 60, 62, 76
Alfred 51, 52
alienation 24, 25, 26, 27, 46
alternatives 29, 58, 61, 62
amendment 12, 13, 30
American 12, 14, 17, 18, 21, 22, 23, 24, 25, 41, 42, 44,
    46, 47, 51, 53, 54, 56, 58, 68, 76, 77, 78, 79, 80, 81,
    82, 83, 84, 85, 86
Americans 5, 16, 17, 18, 26, 33, 57, 58, 65, 69, 77, 83,
    84, 86
analysis 9, 21, 79
annual 14, 77, 78, 79, 80, 81, 82, 83
anti-discrimination 16, 39, 48
anxiety 33, 36, 37, 45, 46, 47, 69, 74
applicants 5, 15, 41, 42, 65, 66
appropriate 33, 36, 37
areas 10, 14, 17, 33, 46, 61, 65, 66, 67, 68, 69, 72, 84
arrests 5, 52, 56, 63
Asian 46, 47, 85, 86
assert 6, 23, 27, 28, 32, 33, 34, 35, 37, 38, 39, 42, 46,
    48, 61, 62, 65, 67, 70, 73, 74, 75
asserts 5, 8, 22, 23, 25, 26, 29, 38, 42, 45
assistance 13, 14, 15, 16, 18, 29, 36, 37, 67, 70
associated 24, 27, 38, 46, 66
association 77, 79, 82, 84, 86
attainment 21, 24, 26, 45
attention 24, 33, 36, 53
attest 32, 33, 44, 70, 73
attorney 54, 56, 58
attorneys 51, 53, 54, 59
autonomy 32, 72, 73, 75

higher 5, 15, 16, 18, 21, 23, 26, 27, 28, 29, 30, 35, 36,
    37, 38, 43, 44, 47, 53, 54, 55, 56, 57, 59, 60, 65, 66,
    67, 68, 73, 75, 76, 85
highlight 17, 26, 53, 60
highlighting 5, 8, 32, 33, 54
highlights 9, 12, 24, 28, 36, 41, 42, 44, 47, 54, 55, 57, 69
hinder 21, 26, 32, 35, 37, 41, 44, 54, 61, 68
hindering 9, 24, 26, 28, 37, 42, 45, 60, 66
hiring 5, 13, 16, 41, 42, 44, 45, 48, 74
historical 2, 5, 8, 9, 12, 16, 21, 22, 23, 24, 26, 32, 37, 41,
    42, 45, 57, 65, 67, 76
historically 16, 66, 67, 68, 80
histories 25, 26, 29
history 14, 17, 21, 24, 26, 32, 55, 56, 58, 73, 81, 83, 84,
    86
home 13, 27, 51, 52, 65, 66, 67, 68, 82
homeownership 65, 66, 67, 70, 80
homes 17, 55, 65, 66, 67, 68
hospital 33, 34, 36
housing 4, 5, 6, 10, 12, 13, 16, 17, 28, 39, 58, 60, 62, 64,
    65, 66, 67, 68, 69, 70, 72, 76, 78, 79, 81, 82, 83, 84,
    85, 86
Howard 21, 24, 25, 80
Howell 34, 35, 36, 80

identify 17, 48, 63, 69, 85
identities 8, 25, 26, 29, 44
identity 8, 9, 15, 37, 44, 73, 78, 82
illness 36, 37, 38
impact 5, 10, 24, 33, 36, 41, 45, 46, 47, 49, 51, 52, 53,
    56, 58, 60, 62, 69, 73, 82, 84, 85
impacts 2, 4, 21, 25, 26, 27, 28, 30, 32, 33, 34, 35, 36,
    37, 41, 46, 51, 52, 54, 57, 60, 65, 67, 69, 73
implement 16, 23, 48, 62, 69
implementing 6, 23, 29, 39, 47, 49, 62
implications 5, 8, 21, 24, 46, 53, 78, 80, 82, 85
implicit 6, 24, 33, 34, 39, 41, 42, 44, 53, 56, 58, 59, 60,
    62, 79, 81, 84
importance 8, 9, 14, 32, 46, 47, 80
improve 14, 15, 28, 38, 39, 60, 62, 67, 70, 80

institutions 5, 6, 8, 9, 10, 13, 15, 19, 21, 23, 25, 27, 29, 45, 48, 51, 74
insurance 18, 32, 33, 35, 37, 38, 65
interactions 9, 33, 34, 35, 37
interest 8, 66, 68, 84
intergenerational 21, 22, 28, 43, 67, 78
intersectional 8, 9, 30, 37, 44, 47
intervention 23, 27, 28, 36, 48, 49, 61
interventions 12, 14, 21, 23, 29, 35, 36, 38, 69, 73, 76, 84
interview 41
investing 6, 23, 28, 30, 39, 48, 49, 74
involvement 14, 24, 57, 61, 74
involves 6, 16, 38, 51, 58, 60, 68, 72
issue 42, 53, 57, 65, 67, 69, 72
issues 12, 13, 14, 23, 29, 32, 35, 39, 46, 47, 54, 57, 58, 59, 61, 66, 67, 68, 69, 73, 81

Jamal 28, 76
Jamal's 28
John 53, 80, 82
Johnson 14, 58, 68, 77, 79, 81
Jones 5, 32, 39, 55, 80, 81
Joseph 44
journal 76, 77, 78, 79, 80, 81, 82, 83, 84, 85, 86
jurisdictions 17, 53, 62
justice 4, 5, 6, 9, 10, 12, 13, 17, 18, 21, 24, 29, 30, 32, 49, 50, 51, 52, 53, 55, 56, 57, 58, 59, 60, 61, 62, 63, 68, 70, 72, 74, 75, 77, 79, 81, 82, 83, 84, 85, 86

Kiera 24
King 59, 61, 62, 82
knowledge 25, 26, 41, 73
labor 36, 42, 44, 45, 47, 76, 81, 83
lack 22, 23, 25, 26, 27, 32, 35, 37, 38, 39, 41, 42, 43, 44, 45, 53, 58, 59, 60, 66, 67
Ladson-Billings 8, 9, 10, 21, 25, 29, 81
land 70, 78, 79
landmark 12, 14, 17, 21, 68
large 2, 28, 42, 59, 83

press 76, 77, 78, 79, 80, 82, 83, 84, 86
pretrial 54, 55, 62
prevalence 36, 38, 86
primary 16, 17, 19, 22, 33, 34, 55
principles 8, 10, 22, 34
prior 2, 13, 14, 18, 54, 55, 56, 72
prioritize 25, 30, 48, 62, 74
prison 55, 57, 58, 59, 83
private 16, 18, 19, 53, 54, 56, 58, 59, 69, 70
probation 51, 56, 58, 59, 77, 83
probationers 58, 59
problems 47, 66, 82, 83
process 5, 15, 16, 27, 28, 41, 42, 55, 56, 82
processes 5, 8, 30, 39, 41, 42, 43, 45, 74
professional 16, 29, 37, 41, 43, 44, 45, 72, 73, 74, 75, 86
professionals 33, 34, 36, 39, 46, 74, 79, 82
profiling 12, 34, 51, 60, 61
profound 5, 10, 21, 22, 24, 25, 28, 30, 36, 45, 46, 52, 53,
    55, 57, 69
program 15, 19, 69, 76, 80, 86
programs 12, 13, 15, 16, 18, 19, 23, 28, 32, 39, 43, 48,
    49, 51, 58, 59, 60, 61, 62, 69, 70, 73, 74, 75, 78
progress 8, 14, 17, 21, 24, 32, 37, 44, 61, 74, 76, 84
prohibited 12, 13, 18, 67
prohibits 12, 13, 16, 17, 48, 68
project 56, 57, 60, 82, 84
promote 6, 9, 10, 14, 16, 19, 24, 26, 27, 28, 29, 32, 38,
    39, 41, 42, 44, 47, 48, 62, 69, 70, 74
promoting 10, 14, 15, 16, 17, 18, 21, 23, 29, 38, 39, 47,
    48, 49, 67, 68, 69, 73
promotion 13, 41, 42, 44, 45, 74
promotions 42, 44, 46
property 2, 22, 23, 29, 55, 67, 83
prospects 22, 28, 43, 57, 60, 73
protection 12, 13, 14, 30, 68, 69, 78
protections 12, 17, 41, 43, 48, 68
provide 8, 18, 22, 23, 36, 39, 48, 49, 52, 53, 54, 61, 62,
    69, 70, 73, 74, 75
providers 5, 33, 34, 35, 36, 37, 38, 39, 60
provides 9, 10, 14, 15, 16, 21, 35, 39, 72